Rhododendrons

and Azaleas

for your garden

Christopher Fairweather

FLORAPRINT LIMITED, PARK ROAD, CALVERTON, NOTTINGHAM.

ISBN 0 903001 37 3

© ÉDITIONS FLORAISSE 1979, ANTONY - FRANCE.

Christopher Fairweather's interest and enthusiasm for rhododendrons and azaleas begun in the early 1950s when he spent two years at Exbury Gardens.

To any serious gardener, Exbury Gardens, near Beaulieu in Hampshire, is synonymous with the breeding and production of high quality rhododendron and azalea hybrids.

He subsequently passed several years in Kenya engaged in various farming enterprises, returning to England in 1960. At this time, he started his own garden centre business in Beaulieu.

In 1968, Mr Fairweather rejoined Exbury Gardens as manager, working at the gardens until 1974. During this time, he was fortunate to have the opportunity of studying rhododendrons, azaleas and camellias, not only at Exbury, but in many parts of the world.

1974 saw his return to his own business, which has now expanded to include an additional garden centre and a ten-acre tree and shrub nursery.

The Author would like to thank Ann Bonar BSc (Hort.) and Christopher Browne for their help and advice.

The Author and Publisher wish to thank Michael Warren for his excellent photographic work and to express their appreciation in being allowed to take photographs at the following gardens :

Exbury Gardens, Hampshire (Edmund L. de Rothschild Esq.).

Felcourt, Copdock, Suffolk (E. F. Allen, Esq.).

Hillier Gardens and Arboretum, Ampfield, Hampshire (Hampshire County Council).

Le Vastérival, Princesse Sturdza, 76119 Varengeville sur mer, near Dieppe.

Manoir de Lanniron, Quimper - France. (M. A. de Massol de Rebetz).

Mc Penny Nurseries, Bransgore, Hampshire (T. Lowndes Esq.).

Parc Départemental de Trévarez, Saint-Goazec par Châteauneuf du Faou - France.

Pépinières Croux, 92290 Châtenay-Malabry - France, for their advice and help with the pictures on pages 3, 45, 53, 68 and 90.

Pépinières Thoby - France, (photos. Chantreau) who has kindly lent us the camellia photographs on pages 113, 115, 118, 122, 123, 124.

Royal Horticultural Society, Wisley, Surrey (The Director).

Savill and Valley Gardens, Windsor Great Park (Crown Estate Commissioners).

Spinners, Boldre, Hampshire (P. G. G. Chappell Esq.).

Stonard, Stoney Cross, Hampshire (P. Hitchcock Esq.).

Stour Valley Gardens, East Bergholt, Suffolk (Mr and Mrs J. H. Gill).

Sutton House, Stutton, Suffolk (F. H. Ridley Esq.).

FRONT COVER :
Soft pink flowers on the early flowering Rhododendron 'Christmas Cheer'.

INSIDE FRONT COVER :
The striking effect of a well established hardy hybrid rhododendron.

Contents

If we were to imagine a social scale in our garden, there is no doubt rhododendrons, azaleas and camellias would come out as the aristocrats. They have a grandeur and fascination unique in the plant world. Years ago they were exclusive to the large gardens of the wealthy and this has contributed to their status. The very word rhododendron conjures up a vision of conspicuous and exotic red and pink flowers appearing in the warmth of spring. This accords well with the meaning of the name (in Greek, rose tree). The majority of gardeners may recognise by name no more than five or six kinds ('Pink Pearl' and 'Britannia' being the best known, apart of course from that woodland weed Rhododendron ponticum). In fact, there are many thousands of different rhododendrons, varying from prostrate alpine plants up to 15 m (50 ft) giants. Colours range from white and yellow through to deep purple, with a flowering period from December to the end of the summer. Azaleas are included botanically in the same genus, which is divided into several groups including evergreen and deciduous varieties. Their range of colour is similar to rhododendrons except for the lack of purple, and a very high proportion of yellow and orange can be found in the deciduous varieties. Camellias are definitely one of the most exotic garden shrubs. Not related to rhododendrons or azaleas, they belong in fact to the same family of plants from which we get our tea to drink. With its neat, glossy leaves and large, waxy flowers, a camellia is always a point of interest in the garden. Not many years ago, these plants were confined to the conservatory and considered too tender to grow outside. In fact, allowing some protection for the flowers, camellias will survive the winter in most gardens. Rhododendrons, azaleas and camellias have had many books devoted to them; a lot of these were full of recondite information put together for specialists. A different kind of book is required by the intelligent person whose enthusiasm for gardening generally has become deep enough to give these fine subjects a certain degree of special attention. Nursery lists, which so often illuminate many garden questions, might be expected to be useful. Here, however, they cast conflicting shadows of uncertainty. The logic of alphabetical listing throws together such wholly dissimilar plants. And the botanical classification is exceptionally tangled in our chosen field : Series and Subseries are added to the usual nomenclature of genera and species in the rhododendron group. Some fancy propagators avoid this heaviness and make their catalogues frothy with high-flown praise of new varieties which they have on exclusive offer. Sometimes we are distracted completely from the practical question, whether the plant is going to do any good in our garden ! This latter question has been taken as the key to this book. The various available kinds are considered according to the different uses to which they can be put. There are lists on the small garden, woodland glade, town garden, rock garden, etc. Which of these will be helpful to you ? Don't forget that a single piece of property can include different situations. For example, a small mixed garden may include a rock garden. Or a larger site may provide a formal layout around the approach to the house, and a shrub border to the side or a woodland area further removed from the buildings. Thus, by taking careful thought, you may be able to draw cleverly upon these plants to produce a wide range of striking effects.

Opposite page :
Arboreum on hillside
above Basonteur, E. Nepal.

Rhododendrons and Azaleas

The origin and history of rhododendrons

From an evolutionary point of view, the Rhododendrons seem to descend from the ancestors of the Magnolias, by way of plants allied to Camellias.

Their heritage immediately places them among the great producers of showy flowers. This has so much to do with their desirability as garden plants that it is surprising to learn that this emphasis on profusion of flowers leads botanists to regard them as somewhat of a primitive example of a flowering plant. Certainly they have existed for a very long time, and fossils are found from fifty million years ago which correspond closely with species still existing in nature.

The indications of these fossils, and the location of the most basic forms of wild Rhododendrons existing today, suggest that this type of plant first arose in the Himalayan regions. It proved very adaptable in the range of types which the genus was to produce, in the sizes of the individual plants, in the number of species, in their dominance very often of the local plant ecology where they thrive, and in their wide distribution around the world.

Geographical distribution

Apart from New Guinea and Indonesia, which are almost on the Equator and have altogether about 200 varieties, and the northern-most tip of Australia to which a single variety extends, Rhododendrons belong to the Northern Hemisphere. There are getting on for a thousand known wild varieties and, apart from reclassification, it is likely that a good many more will eventually be found. The greatest profusion of varieties in any one place is among the mountains of Southwest China, through the border area with Tibet and Burma into Assam and Nepal. Northern China has relatively few, and northern Siberia fewer still, but the significance of these is the connection via Alaska with the Rhododendron population of North America.

This extends right across Canada and down through the United States both by the West coast to California and via the Eastern region to the Gulf of Mexico. The significance of this is, that certain varieties from the Deep South, especially *R. catawbiense* provided the basis for the key steps in hybridization.

The introduction of rhododendrons to Britain

In the Greek, 'Rhododendron', meaning 'rose tree', was a name first applied to the Oleander, and it continued to apply to that shrub of the Eastern Mediterranean until the 16th century. The same period is about the earliest that one finds mention of any plant to which the name Rhododendron now applies. This is because the European member of the genus belong to high altitudes. Until that time mountains were thought of as terrible and frightening wildernesses where nothing desirable was to be found.

But as the Alps lost their terror, their botanical life came to be considered and *Rhododendron ferrugineum* began to appear in the Herbal books. It was entered not under that name, but under various others, with long and confusing descriptions in Latin which did little to clarify matters for the students of those days.

Karl Linnaeus, a Dutch botanist, established in 1753 the categorization of plants which is still used today.

His genus of Rhododendrons contained five species, one of which, *R. chamaecistus,* has been redesignated *Rhodothamnus chamaecistus.*

He proposed a separate genus for azaleas, with six species, of which five have since been included for classification among Rhododendrons and "Azalea procumbens" has been removed and redenominated Loiseleuria procumbens.

Thus, of the over 800 species now known, only nine were named and described by Linnaeus and not all of those had been brought under cultivation anywhere.

The first to be introduced into Britain was *R. hirsutum.*

This happened in 1656, about a century before the arrival of *R. ferrugineum,* its close relative, with the name of 'Alpine Rose'. Its home is above the coniferous tree-line on the Eastern Alps and, at similar altitudes in Transylvania. Its capacity to withstand more alkalinity in the soil than almost any other Rhododendron may have been the secret of its succeeding in cultivation before soil-chemistry began to be understood.

The first American species were Azaleas brought to Britain as seed in 1734. These would appear to have been *R. viscosum* and *R. calendulaceum.* In 1736 came *R. maximum,* the most widespread wild Rhododendron of the eastern United States and known from the region in which it flourished most luxuriantly (becoming a tree reaching to 12 m - 40 ft) as the 'Rosebay of the Carolians'. It is not much cultivated, as great space is needed to accommodate such a large, coarse plant, and it has little show of bloom.

The next Rhododendron to be introduced into cultivation, *Rhododendron ponticum,* was brought to England from Gibraltar in 1763. It had been found there not many years before, after the species had already been named for the "Pontic" region of its first discovery in what is now Turkey.

This plant has naturalised so well in England as to become in places practically a weed. But it compensates for its vigorous intrusion with a very fine and generous display of flowers.

The start of hybridization

Only about a dozen species were in cultivation by the end of the 18 th century, and no hybridization between them had been done. This situation was soon to change, for the next thirty years brought in about twenty new species including the very ones on which hybridization was most to depend. These included *R. caucasicum* from central Asia in 1803, *R. catawbiense* from the Great Smoky mountains of North Carolina, 1809 and *R. arboreum* from the Indian foothills of the Himalayas in 1811. Also, the *Azalea R. molle* came from China, in 1823, to become the parent of the so called *Mollis hybrids.*

The purpose of hybridization may need to be explained. Considering the number of Rhododendron species now available (the best part of a thousand) it might be thought unnecessary to take great trouble (which it does) to generate several thousand more kinds. The confused and evergrowing list of hybrids so far produced probably amounts to about 8,000, which could be deemed absurdly large. Yet something had to be done if the best was to be made of the exciting possibilities of these plants.

Only a couple of hundred species are truly cultivable without alteration. Of these, only a small proportion present an attractive appearance without improvement.

Hybridization aims to combine the best of appearance with the best of growing characteristics. To take an example, the size and colour of the flowers of 'Lady Eleanor Cathcart' come from *Rhododendron arboreum;* but that species is too tender for our climate, so its glories are captured for us by combining that stock with the hardy *R. maximum.*

There might seem to be a difficulty, in that the latter species' hardiness depends on its later-flowering: if they don't flower together, how can two plants be crossed at all ? In fact there are all sorts of tricks for persuading them to bring on or hold back their flowering sufficiently to bring about fertilization with the intended partner. Deliberate hybridization also requires care to be taken to ensure that no fertilization takes place with any partner other than the intended. This is normally done by keeping the flower neatly parcelled up from when it is a tightly closed bud until the seed is safely set except for the moment of introduction of the selected pollen. Even without seeing this done you can easily guess how much time and trouble must be taken to effect a predetermined crossing in such a way, afterwards collecting any seed, sowing it, raising the seedlings, bringing them on to flowering maturity, testing and recording their qualities, and only then being able to see whether all this effort has produced some sort of result.

The first hybridization was accidental: a rare and accidental crossing between the *R. nudiflorum* a deciduous Azalea and the evergreen *Rhododendron ponticum.* The resulting *R. hybridum* was added to the collection of the Royal Botanical Garden at Edinburgh in 1814. There are other "Azaleodendrons" which have been produced by the crossing of different Azalea and Rhododendron partners but very few have been much cultivated. It has seemed more rewarding of effort to try to intensify the best characteristics of fine plants rather than confuse them with those which were too diverse.

At the very time when that Azaleodendron came into being, a Surrey nurseryman named Michael Waterer was beginning on the deliberate hybridization of the two American importations: a pink-flowered form of *R. maximum* with *R. catawbiense*.

(Presumably to have a large plant on which pink flowers would bloom before the year's new growth would hide them). But unfortunately the product of this work in 1810 is now untraceable, if not lost entirely.

Still in the same period, that first specimen of *R. arboreum* which had arrived in Britain in 1811 finally blossomed in 1825. The world of gardening was astounded. The size and globular/shape of the trusses of blooms, the number and size of the flowers they contained and above all the pure crimson colour... in every way it surpassed anything seen before.

The snag was that this plant came from tropical India. Admittedly it grew at an altitude of between five and ten thousand feet, but even so it was not accustomed to frost or cold winds, and it bloomed too early to be out of danger anywhere except on the extreme west coast. Something had to be done to make this exotic colour safe from the rigours of a British winter.

So in the next year was produced a cross of *R. arboreum* with an already existing hybrid of *R. catawbiense* × *R. ponticum*. The result of this was named 'Altaclarense' a Latin translation of 'Highclere' the name of the seat of the Earl of Caernarvon in Berkshire.

This plant, 'Altaclarense', which is still to be found in some gardens, was closely followed by other famous hybrids between the new Eastern importations and the range of species already cultivated in England.

Notable among these were M. Waterer's production. *R. Nobleanum (caucasicum × arboreum)* and *R. Russellianum (catawbiense × arboreum)*. Recrossing of such hybrids with their parental species was also done to intensify their characteristics.

These plants were very much to the taste of 19th century garden lovers, because there had been important changes in the trend of landscape design.

The great parks laid out in the 18th century were intended to show off their handsome character and great extent, and the good husbandry of their owners. But now the wealth of the old landed gentry was declining and there was arising a new brand of wealthy man. He had his business of trading or banking or manufacture somewhere in the city, but his home, where he would raise his family and entertain his friends and take his ease, would be some convenient distance out of town. There he would have a fine house with a garden but no estate. In order that such a garden should seem complete in itself and not too much overlooked by neighbours, there was need of evergreens to close the view. These would be dark, which was a circumstance not difficult to accept for a society so accustomed to wear clothes of black material, but they wanted enlivening; vivid flowers were just the thing.

The expansion of horizons with the growth of Empire made the most exotic extravagances of bloom that could be produced very acceptable.

They were very fashion-conscious people, and a glance at the fashion plates of the period is enough to indicate how perfectly the massive trusses of intense-coloured, frilly blossoms against a dark background were calculated to appeal to their eye and make the Rhododendron perhaps the greatest expression of their taste in the plant kingdom.

Being a badge of wealth and a matter of fashion, of course the latest and best hybrids were highly prized.

An atmosphere of secrecy and intrigue came to surround the experiments for their production, almost like that over the 'Black Tulip' of Alexandre Dumas' novel. The recipe for the parentage of any new type was almost as jealously preserved as the specimen itself. The traces of this anxiety still show in modern Rhododendron lists.

The early hybrids, especially those by the Waterer family, are not fully described as regards their parentage. For example, Doncaster, produced in 1865, is described only as "Arboreum X". That much of its origin is perfectly obvious, the only mysteries being the identity of the other parent and whether arboreum was as usual the male partner.

This deliberate mystery is annoying to us, especially as it generated a tradition of muddled identity among the hybrids of an already confusing and prolific genus. However, one feels the Waterers can be forgiven their part in this because so many members of that family played a positive role in the improvement of stocks. They owned two separate nurseries, of which the original one at Knaphill, near Woking in Surrey, was run successively by two Michael Waterers and then two Johns. At the Bagshot establishment were two Anthonys and then Gomer, who eventually returned to Knaphill. Their successful Rhododendron hybrids, which must number in scores, include *Nobleanum* and *pulcherrimum* (both 1835), 'Mme Carvalho', 'Mrs R. S. Holford' and 'Sappho' (all 1866), 'Pink Pearl' (1897), 'Gomer Waterer' (1900), 'Alice' (1910) and 'Lady E. Cathcart' (1926).

Being already on the subject of the Waterers, this would seem to be the moment to mention the "Knap Hill Azaleas". The work of generations at that nursery went into the crossing and recrossing of at least seven azalea species from different parts of the world.

Innumerable types of large-bloomed, scented and vigorously-growing deciduous azaleas were brought into being, yet not for three quarters of a century did the results publicly emerge. The fruits of this work were at last made known in 1925, and soon the vegetative propagation of these highly-acclaimed plants enabled them to be put on the market.

Lionel de Rothschild, another notable name in the annals of Rhododendron history, owned vast oak-shaded gardens at Exbury, on the Solent side of the New Forest, where he continued the development of the Knap Hill strains with a fresh inventiveness.

As a result, the Knap Hill and "Exbury azaleas" together total over a hundred different registrations with the Royal Horticultural Society and cover, with great brilliance, the entire colour-range of which these plants seem to be capable. The development of these magnificent hybrids is a story of the 1930s continuing well after the second world war; all which, and more, is chronicled in the Rothschild Rhododendron book by Peter Barber and Brigadier Lucas Phillips.

The search for new species

To return to the latter part of the century, the next development after the enthusiasm for hybridization of the already-known species, was a phase of botanical exploration in search of new ones. This is an even more extraordinary and exciting story, well worthy of a book to itself.

Around 1850 mainly from the sikkim on India's northern frontier, Sir Joseph Hooker brought back forty-five new species. These included *Rhododendron Campylocarpum, Rhododendron Wightii, Rhododendron Thomsonii.* The latter species in particular, flowering in 1857, gave impetus to fresh efforts of both hybridization and exploration. Another key plant for further development was *Rhododendron Fortunei,* sent back as seed in 1856 from China by Robert Fortune: apart from the race of hybrids offspring it produced, it proved hardy in the North-eastern United States as well as in Britain. Another batch of discoveries was made by French missionaries around 1880, but the plants themselves, *Rhododendron Delavayi, Davidii, Fargesii, Soothii,* were not grown in Europe until much later.

Dr. Augustine Henry did get his wonderful blue *Rhododendron Augustinii* introduced more promptly however, and *Rhododendron racemosum* was seen here in 1893.

The total of known species at the turn of the 20th century was around 300 of which little more than a tenth were in cultivation. The majority of the unused species that had been described (over 200 in fact) were natives of New Guinea. There was virtually no hope for the cultivation of any such equatorial kinds of plant in temperate lands like Britain except in wholly artificial conditions. But there remained until this time the greatest treasure house of all for rhododendrons, to be discovered in the mountainous hinterland of S. E. Asia.

E. H. Wilson set out in 1899 on the first of four expeditions to China, as a plant collector on behalf of the English Nurserymen James Veitch & Sons, and within two years he had sent back nearly forty new species. His discoveries over a period of twenty years included many Rhododendrons one might today call indispensable, from the large fragrant white *Rhododendron discolor,* to the small, neat *Rhododendron Williamsianum* with its pink bells, the parent of so many modern hybrids.

Likewise George Forrest, starting in 1904 — and dying on his seventh expedition to the interior of China in 1932 — introduced a grand total of 260 previously unknown species. Reginald Farrer also died in the course of an expedition, having spent the best part of six years in China and upper Burma. Captain F. Kingdon Ward began collecting in 1911 in Western China, afterwards veering deeper into Tibet, Assam and Burma. His finds included two of the most spectacular yellows : the beautiful *Wardii* and the huge-leafed *Rhododendron macabeanum;* but also the dwarf pink *R. pemakoense* and the scarlet *Rhododendron Elliottii,* both good garden species.

Other great names could be added to the list of the plant discoveries of this area, for example Rock, Ludlow and Sherriff. Between them all they brought to light more than 600 fresh species of Rhododendrons and also gave the world an inspiring example by their quests, and excitement in their wonderful accounts of the natural glories of almost inaccessible lands.

Rhododendrons, azaleas and camellias in the garden

A group of well chosen evergreen azaleas.

Size and growth

The question most often asked is, how tall will they grow? This applies to Rhododendrons, because there is not too much worry about being overgrown by Azaleas or Camellias. The latter can become trees of 6 m (20 ft) in ideal conditions, after a very long time indeed — but they lose density as they gain height, and never spread sideways in a heavy manner. Japanese Azaleas seldom rise above 1.2 or 1.5 m (4 or 5 ft) tall. Deciduous ones get somewhat taller if neglected on good soil, and could form a thicket of 3 m (10 ft), but there is no need to let that happen.

With Rhododendrons, potential plant size is the most important factor we wish to know. It is the key to their successful use in small gardens. And the setting of planting distances which allow correctly for development avoids wasteful expense. The hereditary character of plants requires us to choose wisely

That warning is really self-evident, but perhaps the next is not. Please don't forget, as many do when they choose a young plant, that you should not demand the luxury of too many flowers in the first season.

It is far better to have a healthy shrub in future than too many flower buds now, and a profusion of bloom on a young plant will restrict growth. Allow it to get well established, and then enjoy the flowers. Can one avoid the delay by buying a plant that is already old enough to be blooming ? This also has its drawbacks. The young vigorous plant will often grow away better after transplanting than a more mature specimen. There is no substitute for patience in gardening.

Climate

The plants we grow in our garden have arrived from all over the world, often originating in climates very much warmer than Europe. In consequence many of the more exotic types, of Rhododendrons particularly, can only be grown in England in the mild southern counties. There are also some western localities in Scotland and Ireland where conditions are made favourable by the influence of the Gulf Stream. In the colder areas it is possible to give extra protection by planting under light shade or having substantial windbreaks around your garden.

To enable you to choose plants that will be hardy in your particular site, I have indicated on each Rhododendron in this book the hardiness rating as used by the Royal Horticultural Society. The explanations of this and the symbols used for it will be found at the beginning of the sections illustrating and describing the species and hybrids.

How and where and when to buy your plants

All the plants described in this book are fairly slow to produce, taking three to four years to reach a good saleable size. Also, propagation can be difficult, so they will be among the more expensive plants you buy for your garden. Therefore, it is important that you make absolutely sure that you buy only the

among the range which extends from miniature species to massive, spreading trees. At the same time, eventual height and rate of growth are, of course, governed by the conditions under which your shrub is growing.

Rhododendrons, like Azaleas and Camellias, enjoy sundappled shade to grow to perfection. Given a soil rich in humus that does not dry out, and if the site is not too exposed, then we can expect surprisingly rapid growth in a range of shrubs that are usually considered slow. It is not unusual for a Rhododendron of the larger type to grow up to 45 cm (1 1/2 ft) in one season given optimum conditions, but if the soil is poor and dry and the site is exposed then growth is reduced to 4 or 5 cm (1 or 2 in) each year. Obviously, do not rely on poor conditions as a means of avoiding overgrowth. You can't expect much beauty from your unhappy plant if you poison, blast or starve it to rectify a wrong choice of variety !

very best specimens, correctly identified by name and free of any disease. As these plants will give you many years of pleasure, it is unwise to buy cheap or inferior plants. So often, a cheap buy can prove to be a poor investment, giving uncertain flowers and little growth, occupying space and wasting time.

There are a number of excellent specialist retail nurseries who would supply your plants. Or perhaps your most convenient solution is to visit your local garden centre and choose the very plant you want.

As the majority of plants sold at garden centres are now offered in pots or containers, it is possible to buy and plant during all months of the year.

Rhododendrons and Azaleas can almost be described as furniture to be moved around the garden during any month of the year. With care and attention they can even be moved in full flower. This is primarily due to a very fibrous and compact root system, but the optimum time to buy a plant is from October to April. Avoid planting when the ground is very dry or during a spell of frost. If weather conditions are not good for planting, keep the plant under cover where, if watered, it can stay for many weeks until things improve. Again, I would like to repeat the warning not necessarily to choose a plant covered with buds. Of course you want to see the flowers as soon as possible but we ask too much of our young plants to expect a mass of flowers and vigorous growth at the same time. Allow the plant to grow first, and the flowers will follow later.

General preparation

The first stage of preparation ought to be planning.

Lots of people leave this out, and some don't even realise that such a thing exists. Garden design is in fact an art, which has its own experts and is of course the subject of other books.

Let us assume you have got your plans about the broad layout of the garden. The rest of the book will help you to decide what part Rhododendrons, Azaleas and Camellias are to play within the scheme, and to know which types are suitable and how to site them.

When both the position and the plant are chosen, we must give thought to getting the one ready to receive the other.

Avoid definite frost pockets. These are places where freezing air is trapped, in its natural tendency to pour downhill like water, by walls, close-set trees, dense vegetation or an actual dip or hollow in the shape of the ground. Frost will not kill suitably hardy plants;

nor will frost alone spoil the early blooms, but when these are hit by the direct rays of the sun with ice-crystals still on them, the result is always sad, brown flowers. Camellias and early-flowering Rhododendrons should be placed out of the early morning sun, and of course it is no use sheltering them with deciduous plants which will be leafless in March.

Soil preparation

Rhododendrons, Azaleas and Camellias will last for many years and give continual colour and enjoyment, therefore every effort should be made to prepare the soil before you plant. I have seen so many sad looking plants in various gardens that will really never make satisfactory specimens, primarily because no proper preparation was made beforehand.

Make sure that the site is well drained. Plants sitting in very wet soil for months on end will become sad and pale, making very little growth. Chronic excess of moisture should be led away in land-drains, and the proper time for installing these is after deciding the garden layout and before cultivation for planting.

Moss growing on the soil is quite a definitive indication of bad drainage, and rushes are still worse. A general idea of the condition of the soil in this respect can be gained just by here and there digging up a lump of soil and squeezing it. If it squashes into a paste from which you can press water out, that is bad, but if it feels crumbly it is in a good state. If it is granular and sandy, it may even be too dry. In that case, the plants you put into it may one day suffer from drought, unless you can supply plenty of water and mulch.

Remember that the fault of badly drained soil lies in its exclusion of air, so that the micro-organisms, which ought to have kept the soil alive and healthy, are drowned.

Heavy clay is to be avoided too, for the same general reason. Often, the sticky wetness and density of such soil is overcome by improving the texture with the addition of plenty of suitable materials such as peat, leaf mould or spent hops. Beware of unexpected small patches of clay in a garden of otherwise suitable soil.

These may have been left by builders' excavations, even years ago, alongside the trenching out of sewer pipes or foundations. Even if there is less than a bucketful of the stuff, the plant you plonk in the middle of it, is going to have an uncomfortable time.

The same sort of local difficulty, only more so, comes when what the builders have left in a particular spot is lime mortar or plaster. The plants we are dealing with all require rather acid conditions. In fact, **you will not be able to grow any of our subjects if there is lime in the soil.** Where this problem exists, it may not be easy to eliminate, and in extreme cases not even worthwhile. In some regions, for instance, the entire soil is heavily charged with lime, and in such situations, success with these plants depends upon their isolation from it.

Lime leaches downhill, so the installation of Rhododendrons in small individual pits filled with acid soil will not necessarily safeguard them in the long term against reinfusion with lime from the surroundings. However, a hummock of limefree soil will remain limefree. The obvious application of this fact is to the rock garden. This way you can grow lime-hating plants on top of a whole downland of chalk!

Clearly we need to know whether the problem of alkalinity exists in our garden before spending money on plants. And if there is a problem it may vary in degree in different parts of the site. Soil can change its character almost from one spadeful to the next.

Even where the builders are not to blame, as mentioned above, there can be strongly localized geological differences. How shall we find out about all this?

Professional firms can perform a soil-analysis for you, but their fees will be very expensive. You can do it quite well yourself. Kits can be bought at any good garden centre for a price you will find well justified by the long-term success of the most treasured specimens in your garden. And you can make sure of taking readings from each exact spot where you want to place one.

The operation consists of comparing with a graduated colour-scale the colour of the solution in your test tube containing the soil sample shaken with distilled water and the indicator-additive. Readings of the acid/alkaline value are taken in the form of the 'pH' number.

This refers to the quantity of hydrogen ions dissolved in the moisture of the soil, but there is no need to go into the chemistry of it. All you need to know is that, while pH 7.0 is chemically neutral, typical garden soil is slightly acid, averaging say pH 6.0. And the proper value for growing our subjects is still more on the acid side, towards pH 5.0. Above pH 6.0, don't grow these plants.

Some adjustment of the chemistry of the soil is possible. Plentiful addition of peat can improve the acidity as well as the structure of the soil, but not extensively.

Sulphur is a more powerful corrective. It should be applied, in the form of either flowers of sulphur or sulphate of ammonia, and, at the rate of 70 g per sq.m. (2 oz per sq yd), it should produce a fall in pH of 3/4 of a point. Distribution must be uniform over the area.

At best, this is a tricky business, and don't forget that the effect of such a chemical adjustment is not permanent. Gradually, according to the soil conditions and drainage, the sulphur acids will leach away, and unneutralized lime, if it was originally present, will return. Restoring, the correction is less simple than making it in the first place was, because you now have established plants to beware of damaging.

All Rhododendrons, Azaleas and Camellias will benefi[t] from a liberal dressing of peat mixed with the soil in an[d] around the planting hole.

Planting technique

Planting can really be carried on throughout the yea[r] — even, with care, when the subject is in full flower. Bu[t] it is a critical operation for the future success of the specimen, and to achieve the very best results I woul[d] advise planting in the early autumn as being mos[t] satisfactory. If this is not possible, the spring would b[e] second choice. The main disadvantage of spring is th[e] seasonal danger of dry winds and occasional drough[t] which can cause all evergreens to suffer, especiall[y] those recently planted.

Basically all our subjects are fibrous rooted and requir[e] a well drained soil that has a high humus content. I[f] you are fortunate enough to have a woodland garde[n] with adequate peat, then further humus is not required[.]

For most gardens a liberal dressing of moss or sedg[e] peat, or leaf mould (ideally from beech or oak), or pin[e] needles can help to open up the soil, and this materia[l] should be worked into the general soil of the plantin[g] area.

Assuming that the ground is now prepared, wit[h] sufficient humus, no lime, no waterlogging bu[t] adequate rainfall to maintain moist roots, then th[e] plant will really require no fertilizer at all. But it can b[e] beneficial at planting time to give the shrubs a littl[e] help to become established quickly and to make goo[d] any deficiencies in your soil.

The top of the root ball should be level with the surface.
Don't plant too deep.

Water in well.

The majority of chemical fertilizers contain varying proportions of nitrogen, phosphorus and potassium compounds, usually written N, P and K respectively. Nitrogen has the effect of promoting green growth, and should only be applied, sparingly, during the spring and early summer. Phosphorus and potassium encourage healthy root-formation and ripen the woody stems of plants ready for the winter, so both are essential to healthy shrubs. If you are planning during the autumn, it will be beneficial to work well into the soil about 70 g per sq m (2 oz per sq yd) each of superphosphate (P) and sulphate of potash (K). For spring planting you can include organic nitrogen (N), and I would recommend 70 g (2 oz) of blood, fish and bone meal per sq m (yd).

Now take out a hole at the planting station similar in size to the root-ball of your plant. Being fibrous-rooted, these subjects must not be planted too deeply. In fact the top of your root-ball should be only a 0.6 - 1 cm (1/4 - 1/2 in) below the existing soil level. Work in your good mixture of soil and humus around the root-ball, ensuring the roots really reach it, but don't press it down too firmly because all our subjects like an open, well-aerated soil. Unless conditions have been really wet while planting, water quite liberally. The plant will be needing extra water for transpiration at this time, and also the water will help settle the soil around its roots. And there's much benefit in putting a little mulch down around the shrub right away.

Watering

Rhododendrons, Azaleas and Camellias all need liberal quantities of water, especially during the growing season. Probably more plants are lost because they become dry during the late spring and summer than from any other cause. The tell-tale sign on Rhododendrons is the drooping and curling of the leaves. This is nature's way of reducing the loss of moisture through the leaves by transpiration. Again, during the winter it is probably the drying effect of cold weather that kills plants more often than the low temperature itself. See that your plants have a really good drink after planting if the ground is at all dry, and make sure that there is plenty of moisture in the soil throughout the year. A mere splash of water may do more harm than good, especially on a hot day.

Evening is the best time to give it.

People worry a lot about using mains-water from the tap to water our lime-hating subjects. It is true that tap water does often contain more lime than we would like, but if you have a naturally acid soil and will not be using tap water continually over many years, it is unlikely you will see any adverse effect.

However, if rainwater is available, it will be slightly acid, rather than alkaline at all, which is ideal.

After care

If there is one secret for growing healthy plants, I believe it is mulching. This is the answer to creating a cool, damp soil, so important to healthy growth. It consists of arranging organic, fibrous material, potential humus not fully decomposed, as a continuous layer or mat, covering the cultivated soil. The plants feed on the slowly rotting vegetation and they get a degree of frost-protection during the winter; also, very important, weeds are suppressed.

Ideally your mulch should be applied in the autumn.

For very young plants, lay it no more than 5 - 6 cm (1 - 1 1/2 in) thick. For more established plants this can be increased to a depth of 15 cm (6 in) or even 30 cm (1 ft). The ideal materials to use are dry bracken (my favourite) or pine needles, or leaf mould. Hop manure and coarse-ground bark are also good.

Moss-peat can be used, but it is not ideal, as it dries too much during hot weather and is then difficult to wet again. Do not use grass-cuttings. These soon rot into a wet, sticky mess and do more harm than good. Also, be careful not to use leaf mould collected from alkaline woodland areas.

Apart from ensuring that your plants are well watered, and free from pests and diseases, after care should be kept to a minimum. Avoid cultivating around your plants because they root right on to the surface, and any disturbance will do damage. If, after the first year, your plants look pale and weak, a light dressing of balanced fertilizer will do no harm. The main thing to remember is to apply sparingly and after planting time, only when required. Healthy established plants require no feed. But don't forget the mulch!

Pruning

It is seldom necessary to prune Rhododendrons and Azaleas, and even less so the Camellias. But they will respond quite happily if the need should arise. Plants do sometimes get leggy and lopsided, or their growth becomes thin and spindly. Again, they can be damaged by falling branches and require fairly drastic reshaping.

Or sometimes in a small garden, it is necessary to keep unduly vigorous varieties within bounds.

Any pruning is best carried out during March, April or May according to the climate. A light pruning consists of shortening each branch that is treated back to a whorl of leaves.

For a more drastic operation, many of the plants can be cut back very hard, and should quickly break away with new fresh growth.

A word of caution: certain Rhododendrons do not respond to drastic pruning, so a certain amount of experimenting may be necessary. The best known hardy hybrid in general use to which this applies is 'Alice'.

Dead heading

This operation really only applies to your best Rhododendrons, and is most important in the case of the young recently planted specimen. As soon as possible after flowering is over, the seedheads should be removed, as shown in the sketch. Be careful to break off the seedhead above the dormant bud. Plants spend considerable energy to produce their seed, and by removing the seed capsule you release this energy and will obtain much improved growth and probably more flower buds for the next year.

Azaleas and Camellias do not really require dead heading. Sometimes one wants to remove flower-heads which are past it, for the sake of appearances only — especially with Camellias.

The seedheads should be removed.

16

Pests and Diseases

Aphids

Of all the plants in your garden these are probably some of the most disease free, but there are one or two insect pests which may give problems which you should look out for. In certain seasons, green aphids can be a nuisance, attacking young, fresh shoots on any of our subjects. Unless steps are taken to destroy this insect, growth will be restricted, and any new shoots will eventually appear very distorted.

Keep a careful watch for this pest in March and April, and spray with malathion or other suitable insecticide to control it if necessary.

Scale Insects

These curious little creatures are mainly seen on the underside of Camellia leaves. Usually, the first signs of trouble are a nasty black sooty deposit appearing on top of the leaves in early summer, and if you look underneath you will see a brown limpet like creature about 0.6 cm (1/4 in) in diameter; they will also be on the bark. Again, spray with malathion or other suitable insecticide, making sure to spray well underneath the leaves. Then, after two or three days when the insects are dead, scrape them off with the back of a knife and wash the sooty deposit off with either warm soapy water or one of the proprietary leaf cleaners.

Rhododendron Fly or Leaf Hopper

An insect that attacks the underside of Rhododendron leaves in late spring and early summer, causing a rather mottled, pale green to yellow effect. Control this again by spraying with a suitable insecticide such as malathion.

Weevils

Grubs (dirty white in colour) of the vine weevil will sometimes attack our subjects just below ground-level and eat all around the bark, which will cause the plant suddenly to collapse and die. If this should happen, dig up the shrub and look carefully at the base of the stem to see if the bark has been damaged.

The grubs make these forays before and after their hibernation, but of course one only becomes aware of it when the plant ought to be preparing to recommence growing.

Counter-measures have to wait until the adult weevils emerge in June, when they attack the leaves, making typical small half-moon shaped cuts as shown in the photograph. The insect is then controlled by spraying or dusting with BHC (HCH) throughout the foliage and also over the surrounding soil. This pest is not widespread in Britain and Europe, but is quite a menace to such plants in America.

Vine Weevil damage.

Bud Blast

Symptoms of this fungus disease are brown to black flower buds with black hairs on them; the buds fail to develop into the hoped-for spring flowers. The best solution on a small scale is to remove and burn the affected material to prevent any further spread. A systemic fungicide such as benomyl (Benlate) is sprayed on to the developing buds in early spring to keep the fungus at bay. It is commonly believed that this infection is spread by insect pests, and so an occasional spray of insecticide in spring is likely to help control where the trouble seems persistent. This complaint is most common on the wild (ponticum) Rhododendron, but fortunately does not yet seem to be too serious amoung our garden varieties.

Galls

These afflict only evergreen Azaleas and certain varieties of dwarf Rhododendron, and come only on young plants less than three years old. Ugly, wart-like growths, red or green in colour, usually first noticeable in springtime, appear singly on leaves, which should be picked off and burnt. The disease spreads by means of fungal spores which the wind and insects carry, but it seldom amounts to a serious complaint. If the plants were to become badly affected, the answer would be to spray them with Bordeaux mixture. Galls are more likely to be found in a very wet season.

Phytophthora

This fungus disease of Rhododendrons and Camellias causes the root and stem to rot. The plant gradually turns pale green, then to brown, and dies. Unfortunately, there is very little that we can do to control this troublesome complaint; the best solution is to remove the plant completely and burn it. Also, do not replace with a similar variety in or near the infected ground.

Other problems

Lichen

Often troublesome on Azaleas, both deciduous and evergreen. Generally the cause is wet and badly-drained soil and lack of plant food, which produces a rather stunted, slow-growing plant. Deciduous varieties can be sprayed on the bark with lime-sulphur in the dormant season. Of course, the evergreen types cannot be sprayed, and the only cure is to scrub off the lichen with a nail brush, soap and water. .
Also, any old and badly affected branches should be cut out. At the same time, prevent recurrence by improvement of the drainage and conditions of your soil by adding humus in the form of peat, leaf mould or pine needles, plus a light balanced dressing of fertilizer in the spring.

Bark-split

This rather English hazard is a matter of being caught out by the weather. The bark of Rhododendron and Azaleas can split badly at the base of the stem when a hard frost occurs in spring (or sometime autumn) while the sap is running. The only defence is to shelter the plants if a dangerously unseasonable frost is forecast. Once the damage has occurred, you must not delay to bind up the wound before it weakens or even kills the plant. Use a strip of clear plastic tape which can be kept on for some months until the split is calloused over. Don't forget to remove the tape when it has done its job, or it may cause its own damage.

Bark split on a young Rhododendron.

Leaf-curl

This is another effect of the weather but not so serious, nor so likely to take you by surprise. During periods of drought, but also during very cold, frosty weather, you will notice that the leaves curl at the edge and droop from the stalk. It occurs to some extent in all our subjects, but most noticeably in the larger-leafed rhododendrons and particularly in specimens recently replanted. The plant is not necessarily suffering, only protecting itself from drying up. This is nature's device to reduce the moisture lost by transpiration. In the winter, there's not much you can do, but in case of drought, obviously a really good drink of water will help.

Propagation

Of all aspects of gardening, the propagation of your own plants is the most fascinating. How satisfying it is to root your own cutting and watch the plant grow and flower! Rhododendrons, Azaleas and Camellias offer quite a challenge to the amateur propagator and the methods by which they can be reproduced include from cuttings, by layering, by grafting and from seed.

Cuttings

Rhododendrons, Azaleas and Camellias can all be rooted from cuttings. These can be taken when the new growth is semi-ripe, which is generally in September or October, except from deciduous azaleas, which yield the best cuttings from fresh, soft growth, in early spring. Shoots 7.5 - 10 cm (3 - 4 in) long, entirely of the current season's growth, are cut, and for the very best results, I suggest you carefully select these only from young and vigorous plants.

It is good to trim off the tips of the leaves to some extent, to reduce the area from which the cutting is losing moisture by transpiration before its roots are grown. Also, a wound made near the cut end increases the area from which roots will spring. This is done by lightly scraping off the surface of the bark for the length of about an inch to expose the cambium, the first green layer. Then the cut end, and this wound, should be dipped into a hormone rooting-compound.

When you wish to take a small number of cuttings these are best put in a seed tray using a mixture of 50 % moss-peat and 50 % sharp sand. Ideally the cuttings should be kept in a greenhouse and covered with a light-gauge polythene, or a plastic lid which is available on many of the small plant propagating boxes you can now buy from your garden centre or horticultural shop.

If in your greenhouse you have a small area heated with a soil-warming tray, try to keep the temperature at the base of your boxed cuttings to 21° C (70° F).

A useful way to take an accurate soil temperature for this purpose is to fill the crack between two cutting boxes with sand into which you thrust the soil-thermometer. It is advisable once every week to give the cuttings a breath of fresh air for about half an hour.

Another wise precaution is to water them every ten days with a solution of a fungicide such as Benlate to prevent any of the fungus problems which occur so easily in a warm, moist atmosphere.

Many cuttings will root in eight to twelve weeks.

When well rooted, put them into a small 7.5 cm (3 in) pot with a mixture of 75 % moss-peat and 25 % sharp sand. A little fertilizer can be added, consisting of 28 g (1 oz) superphosphate, 14 g (1/2 oz) sulphate of potash, 14 g (1/2 oz) sulphate of ammonia and 14 g (1/2 oz) magnesium limestone; these quantities being enough to put with 0.03 cu m (1 cu ft) of potting mixture. Be very careful with the young roots, which are delicate and can easily break off. Also, do not push the mixture down too firmly, as the plants prefer a light, open compost with plenty of air.

Keep the cuttings in a warm, moist atmosphere, until they are really settled in and have started to make new roots in the pot. After this they can be taken outside and kept in a frame until they are ready to go out into your garden. To check on rooting progress, do not be afraid to examine what is going on inside one or two sample pots here and there; tap the upturned pot gently until the contents drop out into your hand for inspection. Remember to keep your young cuttings frequently watered at every stage.

Layering

Rather a slow method of propagation, but definitely a simple one, so if you are content to obtain one or two young plants from one of your favourites, then layering may perhaps be the answer. Choose a branch that is near to the ground, and peg it down as shown in the sketch. It is very important to incorporate plenty of moss-peat and sharp sand into the soil where you are planning to root your plant.

A layered Rhododendron showing how the plant should be pegged.

Layering Rhododendrons, a simple but slow form of propagation.

Seed

Here is another slow but simple method of multiplying Rhododendrons, Azaleas and Camellias. Of course, the plant-breeder is obliged to grow from seed, if he means to produce a new hybrid stock by the crossing of existing forms. But hybrids, when they develop seed, will not necessarily breed true to type. On the contrary, they are very likely to throw back to parental forms. Since the majority of garden forms of all our subjects are hybrids, there is a possibility that the plant you want to reproduce may be one which is only capable of propagation by the three other, foregoing methods.

However, if growing from seed is what you want to try, the fat brown seed-pods should be collected, from about late December through January, dried off thoroughly and broken open to extract the very fine seeds, which are like flakes of tobacco. The seed can be sown in boxes or seed pans in late February or early March — perhaps a little earlier if you have a heated greenhouse. A mixture of fine sifted peat is an excellent sowing medium. The seed should be sprinkled finely on top of this and not covered, but just gently pressed down into the surface of the peat.

A sheet of glass or polythene should cover the pans and make sure they are kept moist and warm, the ideal temperature being about 16 - 18° C (60 - 65° F).

Within a week or two the seed should germinate, then the glass or polythene can be removed and the seedlings will grow away quite quickly. When they are large enough to handle, they should be pricked out, as you would prick out bedding plants, into further boxes containing a mixture of peat with a little sand.

And when they have grown on enough again they can be transferred to a small nursery bed in your garden.

Also, it is useful slightly to wound the bark where the branch is pegged to the ground, and treat the wound if possible with a touch of hormone rooting-compound.

Depending upon various conditions when you carry out this layering — which in fact can be done all year round — it will take from twelve to eighteen months to produce a well-rooted new plant. Once this has got the necessary main root it can be cut from the mother plant, carefully lifted, and planted again where wanted in well-prepared soil. But you need to be very careful when you are doing this moving operation to make sure that the tender, new root does not fall off the old wood from which it has grown.

Grafting

Before we had the modern aids now used in propagation, many of our Rhododendrons were grafted on to the wild *Rhododendron ponticum*. This is a way of providing a robust root-system for a variety which might not grow such a good one on its own. But also, unfortunately, it often results in the troublesome development of suckers which, if neglected, may take control. One sees evidence of this in many old, neglected gardens where the original hybrid Rhododendrons have become completely overwhelmed by their own suckers of the more vigorous, purple-flowered ponticum. If you have any grafted Rhododendrons, keep a sharp eye out for suckers, and pull off any you find carefully at ground level.

Despite modern aids to propagation, quite a number of Rhododendrons are still quite difficult to reproduce and the only effective way is by grafting, which is best carried out during December or January. For the amateur this is a very difficult and precise form of propagation.

Rhododendron suckers should be removed if they grow from the base of a grafted plant.

The suburban garden of between 700 and 1,000 square metres

Azalea Mollis as part of a mixed shrub border.

Let us suppose that your garden consists of various elements, of which one is a range of shrubs; there are many ways in which these can be chosen and used, and every gardener will make his own selection to suit both his personal preferences and the requirements of the site. You can try to borrow some ideas from your neighbours, but your needs will quite possibly be very different; one garden may be in a position where it is exposed to the wind, another may be shaded by large trees, and yet a third over-run by dogs or wild children.

Even the soil can vary over a yard or two, particularly if excavators have worked on it.

Think about the main features of your garden : paths, hedges, clumps of flowers and shrubs, and, most of all,

trees. These are what determine the way the sections of a small garden are arranged, although the house has to be at its centre. As we have seen, their presence is beneficial to Rhododendrons and Azaleas. The factors on which the choice of species depends should be :

1. the fully-grown height and spread (avoid very large trees such as chestnuts, beeches or cedars, for example, which will eventually become a nuisance)

2. the requirements of the roots for water and nutrition

3. the density of shade they will produce

4. their decorative value in all respects, and in particular their bark, foliage, blossom, and autumn colouring.

The contrasting colours of three excellent rhododendrons for the small garden. 'J. Arthur Ivens', 'Elizabeth' *and* 'Dairymaid'.

The silver birch is often chosen; its bark blends admirably with the leaves of Rhododendrons and its light foliage lets enough illumination through. But beware of its spreading roots! The whitebeam and the different varieties of sorbus are recommended (especially *Sorbus aria* 'Lutescens' with its marvellous silver leaves), as well as the other medium-sized trees with coloured leaves; the mass of foliage can be lightened with the yellow of *Robinia pseudoacacia* 'Frisia' or, on the other hand, it can be darkened with the purple leaves of *Prunus cerasifera* 'Nigra', *Malus (tschonoskii)* and *Acer palmatum* 'Atropurpureum'. To obtain flamboyant autumnal colours, you would choose from, among others, the *Prunus sargentii, Liquidambar styraciflua,* Japanese maple or again *Enkianthus campanulatus, Nyssa sylvatica* (scarlet in autumn), *Cercidiphyllum japonicum* and *Amelanchier canadensis* (which also flowers in spring). The *Prunus subhirtella* 'Autumnalis' flowers from November and during the winter, provided it is not caught by frost.

Next to the house the first shrub to plant should perhaps be a Camellia; it will be sheltered by the building and be very useful for decorating your north-facing wall, where few shrubs would be happy.

You can also plant around your door, alongside the steps if there is room, and under the windows, low Rhododendrons and Azaleas (Kurume Azalea would be very suitable, particularly since it is an evergreen) either in beds of the same variety or mixed with other dwarf shrubs or ground cover plants which we shall be looking at later on.

Planting technique is discussed in detail on p. 14 but it is advisable to give a warning at this point to beware of the possible presence in the soil of splashes of wall coverings such as whitewash or, even worse, of builders' rubble with a high content of chalk. The latter warning would apply to the whole of a small garden when the house is of recent construction.

In such a case, dig holes which are much larger than needed for planting, and partially refill them if you find nothing alarming. If, on the other hand, the soil is poor, remove as much of it as possible and replace it with good acid soil and peat. Your plants will not, of course, restrict their growth to the holes in which they are planted. Their roots will spread and it is better to save them from "unfortunate encounters" which could cause them to perish.

Another basic piece of advice which bears repeating : allow sufficient in your budget to ensure good feeding for your shrubs for several years (see page 16), in which case they will develop rapidly. If you spend everything on buying the plants and allow nothing for a mulch for them you may have a greater number of shrubs but none of them will do well and at the first drought you risk unnecessary losses.

Let us now move on to your **bed of Rhododendrons;** it will be more interesting to have a number of different varieties to give a range of colours in the spring, and also to group them with plants which flower at other times. Finally, careful thought must be given to the dimensions of all these shrubs, their habit, whether erect or spreading — or creeping — to enable them to be planted in such a way as to set off the overall mass.

When planting the fairly large Rhododendrons you must of course allow each one enough room for its future growth which, as we have already seen, will reach a width of 2 to 3 m (6 1/2-10 ft) or sometimes more.

But this poses a problem, for when you buy them they rarely measure more than 60 cm (2 ft) high by 50 cm (1 1/2 ft) wide. Shrubs of this size would look a little silly if planted with the generous 4 to 6 m (13-20 ft) spacing they require. There are several solutions :

1. Design your shrubbery as it will be when the plants are fully grown; plant the Rhododendrons in their allotted positions and fill the empty spaces between them with shrubs which you would remove after a few years for re-positioning. This solution implies that you have planned a site for this second group at the appropriate time.

2. Follow the first solution, but fill the gaps with plants destined to be disposed of in due course.

There are many fairly cheap shrubs which grow fast but as time goes on acquire an untidy and unattractive appearance. Shrubs suitable for this type of temporary association include : *Buddleia, Escallonia, Deutzia, Forsythia, Cytisus, Ribes, Kerria, Cornus, Philadelphus.*

In both cases, make sure that the shrubs planted in the spaces cannot hinder in any way the growth of your Rhododendrons.

3. Grow a carpet of ground cover plants between your young Rhododendrons. Be careful with **combinations of colours** when several different shrubs

A spring scene.

Yellow Azalea 'Harvest Moon' with Azalea 'Vuyk's Scarlet' and the soft lavender Azalea 'Iro-hayama'.

Rhododendrons and azaleas growing well together.

are to flower at the same time. Do not use bright colours excessively but blend them with gentler shades and with white : 'Scarlet Wonder', 'Bow Bells', 'Humming Bird', 'Temple Bell' and 'Rotenburg', for example, would make a harmonious group of reds, pinks and white. Take care also not to mix reds which clash, which can happen in spite of what some people may think. This can also occur with various badly matched shades of pink, with some tending towards blue and others towards salmon.

Another piece of advice : do not choose your shrubs solely for their blooms, as these only last a few weeks.

Certain characteristics such as the **decorative effect of young shoots,** for example, will help to prolong the visual interest of your shrubbery. Among the plants worth growing for this reason, the following Rhododendrons can be mentioned :

'Bow Bells'	'Pink Drift'
'Elizabeth Lockheart'	'President Roosevelt'
'Humming Bird'	The variegated *Rhododendron ponticum*
'Impeditum'	
'Moser's Maroon'	'Williamsianum'

To accentuate even more the effect of these young shoots, a few *Pieris* can be placed to good avantage; *Pieris* 'Forrestii' and 'Flame of the Forest' produce brilliant red shoots in early spring; these are followed by small flowers similar to those of the lily-of-the-valley. *Pieris taiwanensis* is particularly notable for the beauty of its clusters of flowers, whereas the variegated-leaved varieties of *Pieris japonica* 'Variegata' provide a different kind of decorative effect.

Others shrubs which may be combined with Rhododendrons

No other medium-sized shrub goes better with the Rhododendron than its relative **the Azaleas**, and in particular the deciduous varieties: in the winter their bare branches give space; in the spring their blooms appear before the foliage and are not, therefore, concealed by it; their foliage is a lighter green in spring, and in the autumn it presents remarkable shades of red and bronze before falling.

Coloured foliage is a major decorative feature. Thus the leaves of *Eleagnus maculata* 'Aurea' with their gold variegation contrast marvellously with the dark green of the Rhododendron foliage; the same applies to *Philadelphus coronarius* 'Aurea', to all the variegated hollies and to some small conifers. Uniform colours can be introduced by means of the dark red foliage of *Berberis thunbergii atropurpurea, Cotinus coggygria* or *Corylus maxima* 'Purpurea', the purple-leaved filbert, and the golden yellow of *Sambucus plumosa* 'Aurea'.

Excessive use should not, however, be made of this coloured foliage at the risk of obtaining too gaudy or "artificial" an overall effect. It is better to use it for two or three splashes of colour among the mass of green foliage, which must remain dominant.

If you wish to have flowers early in the season, why not plant some *Daphne mezereum* in the foreground ? It is very hardy and will be covered with pink flowers (white for the 'Alba' variety) in March and even as early as February; they perfume the air delicately. This shrub will not grow above 1 m (3 ft) approx. Its attractive long bluish leaves appear after the flowers, and its red fruits provide a new attraction in the autumn.

Daphne odora grows taller but is worth growing for its red-tinged white flowers which can appear in the winter if it is not too severe : they perfume your entire garden at a time when you do not expect to come across "spring" fragrances. It is best grown in a mild climate, otherwise it will need a great deal of protection.

Hamamelis mollis is a shrub of remarkable beauty and interest, which will brighten your garden in midwinter and appreciates being grown in similar conditions to the Rhododendron. Its beautiful round deciduous leaves remind one of those of the hazel and take on splendid autumn hues; but it is in winter that the yellow and delicately scented flowers appear on the bare wood. This erect shrub can reach a height of 4 m (13 ft) in time and will form a large, light "fan" shape above the squat rounded outlines of your Rhododendrons.

Of course, **the Camellias** should not be forgotten. They bloom well before Rhododendrons and Azaleas and like similar growing conditions.

The heath *Erica carnea* forms a delightful green carpet all year round, and is covered with white or pink flowers in winter.

R. 'Scarlet Wonder' *and Berberis thunbergii atropurpurea and Philadelphus coronarius* 'Aurea' *give a massed effect.*

Erica arborea 'Alpina' and *Erica lusitanica* are tree heaths over 2 m (6 1/2 ft) tall, which need a lot of shelter but are covered with delicate white blooms in winter. Their effect will be greatest at the rear of your shrubbery under cover of a taller tree which will protect them from frost.

Taking over in **July and August** from the spring flowering species, the *Eucryphia* will be covered in cascading white flowers and will then assume splendid colours in the autumn. Like Rhododendrons, they appreciate soil rich in humus and should be grown in a mild climate. In our country these large shrubs can attain a height of 5 m (16 1/2 ft).

Also in July and August, pleasure is derived from the white flowers of *Stewartia pseudocamellia,* whose foliage also takes on an attractive hue in the autumn. Allow for a fully grown height of about 3 m (10 ft).

Low shrubs are very useful near the house or in front of shrubberies. We have already mentioned the usefulness of *Daphne* and the heathers in this respect. Use can be made of dwarf Rhododendrons and Kurume Azaleas which do not exceed 1 m (3 ft).

Evergreen azalea 'Blue Danube' surrounded by a group of hardy ferns, forming an attractive foliage pattern and excellent ground cover.

The Viburnums, one species of which, the famous "Snowball", is known to everyone, also include a number of very interesting small shrubs such as *Viburnum davidii* which grows no taller than 1 m (3 ft); it is of a rounded shape and covered with splendid, very dark evergreen leaves endowed with veins which give them relief. It has small pinkish white flowers in June and handsome dark blue fruits (drupes) in autumn. It is fairly hardy in Britain.

Viburnum carlesii is of a similar size. Its main interest lies in its round clusters of marvellously fragrant flowers in April and May. Their pinkish-white colour would if necessary soften the brilliance of a red or bright pink Rhododendron blooming at the same time.

One of the best small shrubs is *Skimmia japonica,* which forms a well defined rounded dome not more than 1.5 m (5 ft) approx. high; its male plants bloom as early as February and later, on the female shrubs alone, it has magnificent red berries which birds do not like and which last throughout winter. One male shrub is required for every four or five or so female plants if berries are desired except for the species *Skimmia reevesiana,* which has hermaphrodite flowers (male and female flowers on the same plant).

If you plant **Junipers,** either short or creeping, it is advisable to spread several throughout the shrubbery in order to repeat the effect of their foliage at various places.

Perennials and bulbs

Perennials can be very satisfactorily associated with Rhododendrons and Azaleas, but it is preferable to choose either species which form a carpet or species with a tidy outline which will not risk creating a "jumble" in the shrubbery. They must also be chosen to suit the soil conditions and aspect required by Rhododendrons. With these ideas in mind, and in order to obtain a decorative effect in the various seasons, one may choose in particular: *Hosta* (still called *Funkia* in certain catalogues). These are plants which disappear in the winter but re-appear each spring and last all summer until the frosts, with handsome leaves forming big rounded tufts; with their bluish, yellow or green shades, occasionally variegated with gold or white, they brighten the dark masses of evergreen foliage. *Euphorbia, Helleborus* and ferns are very suitable, as are primulas — including *Primula denticulata* and the Japanese primulas — and the *Meconopsis* with its beautiful flowers which recall those of the poppy but are blue or yellow, depending on the variety.

Bulbs are particularly well suited to an association with Rhododendrons. The mulch which the shrubs need is also an excellent growth medium for them.

I suggest :

Anemones	*Leucojum*
Crocus	Lily
Cyclamen	*Montbretia*
Chionodoxa	*Muscari*
Erythronium	*Scilla*
Iris reticulata	*Trillium* (not to be confused with *Trollius,* which would also be suitable).

Many **ground cover plants** can provide a luxurious carpet between all these plants or simply between the Rhododendrons while waiting for them to grow.

Everyone knows the beautiful effect of the **ivy,** which is very useful in the shade, and its numerous varieties, some of which have variegated leaves. Much pleasure will be given by the charming white flowers of the creeping dogwood or *Cornus canadensis,* the handsome regular foliage of *Pachysandra terminalis,* the delicacy of *Tiarella,* whose dainty stalks of white flowers stand up in the spring above enchanting foliage, and finally by the blue flowers of the periwinkle. It should be remembered too that the heath *Erica carnea* also forms a neat carpet flowering in winter.

These ground cover plants have the big advantage of hiding the soil, which would otherwise have remained bare between two trunks, and of stifling weeds, provided that the soil was not infested with them at the time of planting.

Gardens in Paris.

Rhododendrons, Azaleas and Camellias in the town garden

The main function of a garden in a town is to be looked at from the house and to provide a refuge and a haven of freshness for the eye. The problems which it poses generally arise from its sometimes inconvenient shape and the way in which it is cut off from the outside, often by high walls giving a lot of shade. When empty such a garden may make one think of a box without a lid. To remedy this in summer, a few trees of sufficient size and some well placed shrubs are all that is required, but for more than half of the year one is obliged to rely on evergreens.

Rhododendrons are suitable for this purpose since they mostly tolerate conditions of life in town, and Camellias are even better adapted to this type of situation. When choosing varieties, look for hardy hybrids of a medium size. In a restricted space of this nature, the size of the shrubs is a more important factor than the colour of the flowers.

Another typical characteristic of the town garden is the poor quality of the soil. Its fertility is never renewed by nature, as is the case in the country.

Furthermore it is polluted by particles suspended in the air from toxic fumes and chemical products.

These fall out gradually if they are not brought down by the rain. The "soil" may even be nothing more than an accumulation of waste from urban life, bits of cement, broken glass and scrap iron. On top of all that, if you are lucky, there may be a little earth, but this is probably only clay dug out of the foundations, mixed with bits of ground-up cement. If the soil is in this condition the only solution is to replace it completely. Alternatively one may make do by adding large quantities of peat in order to improve its texture.

The third problem in a town garden is that of shadows thrown by surrounding buildings and perhaps also by already established trees. They take much of the light, which reduces considerably the list of plants which may be grown; water dripping after rain may also be detrimental to some plants.

Happily Rhododendrons generally prefer a certain amount of shade and a sheltered position and will give satisfaction in towns. The darker and shinier their leaves, the better they will resist air pollution.

This is why Azaleas are less happy in an urban situation and Camellias, on the other hand, do well. Good quality blooms, which will last longer than they do in the country, can be obtained. Those who wish to risk growing the more delicate varieties have their chance here; it should be possible to attempt the cultivation of the less hardy varieties of these two species. Satisfactory results should compensate for an unfortunate stroke of bad luck if the winter is very severe or if a late frost occurs.

There are innumerable possibilities for covering the ground with low plants between your shrubs. *Bergenia* and *Hosta* are among the most useful plants, although even more sure and easier results can be obtained with certain Geraniums (not to be confused with the balcony Geranium, which is in reality a *Pelargonium*), and *Alchemilla mollis;* this latter perennial, once established, will thrive and expand without any effort on your part. The same applies to ferns, whose charm remains unequalled.

"Empty" periods can be filled by means of bulbs and annual bedding plants.

Pink Rhododendrons with Big Ben in the background.

A few plants for a town garden

Rhododendrons

'Britannia'	red
'Blue Diamond'	blue
'Baden-Baden'	red
'Carmen'	red
'Curlew'	yellow
'Chikor'	yellow
'Cilpinense'	white tinged with pink
'Christmas Cheer'	pink
'Elizabeth'	red
'Fabia'	orange
'Humming Bird'	red
'Idealist'	yellow tinged with pink
'Pink Drift'	pink
'Rotenburg'	pale yellow
'Sarled'	white
'Seta'	pink
'Williamsianum'	pink

Evergreen Azaleas

'Apple Blossom'	pink and white
'Blue Danube'	mauve
'Blaauw's Pink'	pink
'Hino Crimson'	crimson
'Hinomayo'	pink
'Mother's Day'	red
'Orange Beauty'	deep orange
'Palestrina'	white
'Vuyk's Scarlet'	red

Deciduous Azaleas

'Ballerina'	white
'Berryrose'	pink
'Daviesii'	cream
'Cecile'	deep pink
'Gibraltar'	orange
'Strawberry Ice'	pink
'Pontica'	yellow
'Royal Lodge'	red

Camellias

'Adolphe Audusson'	red
'Apollo'	red
'Anticipation'	pink
'Donation'	pale pink
'Elegans'	pink
'Lady Clare'	pink
'Leonard Mèssel'	pink
'Magnoliiflora'	pale pink
'Preston Rose'	pink
'Francis Hanger	white

R. 'Fastigiatum' with rock, Alyssum saxatile and red saxifrage.

Finally, in good weather the use of the garden may be extended after sunset by means of artificial lighting. In addition to the general overall effect obtained, this lighting enables advantage to be taken of the beauty of plants whose blooms are particularly attractive at night.

The rock garden

Rock gardens seek to reproduce the "natural gardens" found in mountainous, rocky regions. They consist of low plants, conifers, mosses, etc. growing freely among blocks of stone. We are not going to write a treatise here on this vast subject, but it is as well to remember that Rhododendrons are in fact mountain plants and that the dwarf species could not be better suited to this type of application.

A rock garden should not be short of light, although in certain cases it is possible for it to face north if it is well lit; it must at the same time be both well watered and perfectly well drained. Proximity to large trees is not very favourable since rockery plants do not like being covered with dead leaves in the autumn nor being subjected to water dripping from branches after rain.

It is not necessary, and can even be undesirable, to use large quantities of stone. A rockery can be created with a few judiciously placed large stones, which will give a more natural effect than piling up a large heap of stones at the corner of a lawn or of the house. If one is fortunate enough to have a bank or piece of sloping land it will be easy to give the composition some relief, but it is possible to make some very attractive designs on a flat piece of ground. The "effect of relief" may be created by careful arrangement of the plants according to their height, with the tallest on the outside and the lowest ones, mosses and ground cover plants towards the centre. Some well planned gardens create the illusion of a small valley where one can imagine seeing a stream flowing although the ground may be practically flat.

Depending on the overall scale, one may use small shrubs such as *Rhododendron impeditum*, *R. racemosum* or *R.* 'Sapphire', for example, combined with alpine plants which it is impossible to list here as the range of varieties is so great. In a larger scale rockery. Rhododendrons of approx. 1 m (3 ft) in height, Kurume Azaleas, small conifers and heathers, inter alia, can be combined beautifully.

Woodland scene with Rhododendrons Yedoense and triflorum, with 'Cornish Cross' *in the background.*

Small Rhododendrons (1 m to 1.5 m (3-5 ft) approx.)

'Arthur J. Ivens'	pale pink
'Augfast'	lavender blue
'Blue Diamond'	blue
'Blue Tit'	blue
'Pink Drift'	"lavender" pink
'Bo Peep'	primrose yellow
'Cilpinense'	pinkish white with deep pink buds
'Elizabeth'	blood red
'Elizabeth Lockheart'	beetroot red
'Hardize's Beauty'	light pink
'Moonstone'	creamy yellow edged with pink, brown-red buds
'Quaver'	pale yellow
'Remo'	yellow
'Songbird'	deep violet
'Temple Belle'	pale pink
R. tephropeplum	pale pink
	bright pink depending on violet variety
R. williamsianum	pale pink
R. yakushimanum	pink to white

The cold greenhouse or conservatory

These constructions, which protect plants from frost, give us the opportunity to grow certain shrubs to perfection and to take advantage of early flowering. For many years the Camellia was thought of as a greenhouse plant, though we now know that it can flourish in all climates except the harshest.

Nevertheless it is worth growing under glass to have the joy of admiring its marvellous flowers at the peak of perfection in February and the beginning of March, protected from cold winds and spring frosts.

The most delicate varieties of Rhododendrons are particularly well suited to a cold greenhouse. Most have strongly scented uniform white flowers, or white flowers with splashes of pink. Forty or fifty years ago these plants were grown in pots to enable them to be taken into the house, which they perfumed with their delicate fragrance. Certain small Rhododendrons such as 'Moupinense' and 'Cilpinense', can suffer from spring frosts. Under glass their magnificent blooms will still be available for interior decoration.

The Azaleas with large blooms which we buy at Christmas belong to the species *Indica*. They do not tolerate our winters and need protected conditions.

Warmth is required to persuade them to flower in winter. Plant them out in the garden in the summer, do not let them go short of water, and you will be able to keep them for many years. Unfortunately many die fairly early in their life; it may perhaps be wiser to force the blooming of certain dwarf evergreen Azaleas such as 'Blaauw's Pink', 'Hinomayo', 'Hino Crimson' and 'Mother's Day' under glass, which lend themselves to this practice and provide magnificent interior decorations; these varieties have the further advantage of being hardy outside all the year except in a very severe climate. Other than in winter, your cold greenhouse should need no further heating except on certain cold spring days, which are particularly harmful to the flowers.

Explanation

of

symbols

In the notes given in each of the following descriptions of Rhododendrons and Azaleas, a hardiness rating and flower quality indication, as used by the Royal Horticultural Society, are supplied, and also the R. H. S. Awards, as follows.

Hardiness

To express the degree of hardiness, the symbol H has been used, with the numbers 1 to 4 representing the degree. H 4 indicates a hybrid hardy anywhere in the British Isles, which will generally grow in an exposed position. H 3 means hardy in the south and west of England, along the sea-board, and in sheltered inland gardens. H 2 is for a hybrid which requires protection even in the most sheltered garden. H 1 represents a hybrid which can usually be grown only in a greenhouse.

Flower Quality

To help you choose the plants of outstanding flower quality I have again used the Royal Horticultural Society symbols as follows :

F 4 = Excellent flower quality
F 3 = Good
F 2 = Fair
F 1 = Of little merit
❀ = Approximate flowering time

Awards

The Royal Horticultural Society also gives awards to outstanding plants; this can help you choose the best for your garden. The awards are as follows :

FCC = First Class Certificate (the highest award)
AM = Award of Merit
AGM = Award of Garden Merit

The awards are shown for each plant, not in chronological order, but in the order given above.

Hybrid rhododendrons

*A great deal of hybridizing between about half a dozen species of rhododendrons
was done during the last century, and this produced many completely hardy hybrids,
which would grow in exposed conditions without damage,
and which were highly ornamental, both as to leaf and flower. In the early years
of the present century, there was a further great burst of
crossing of the many, many new species then being found and sent back by such plant-
hunters as Forrest, Kingdon-Ward, Wilson, Rock, Ludlow and Sherriff.
These new hybrids were even more scintillating, though some, not many,
need sheltered gardens to do their best. All, however, show an unbelievable range
of colour, flower shape, habit and leaf variation, as can be seen
from the illustrations which follow.*

Rhododendron 'Alice'.

'Alice' (See p. 31)

✿ May   U. H. 3.6 m (12 ft)   F3   H4

Thought by some people to be an improvement on 'Pink Pearl', this hybrid is however, not as large. The clear pink flowers, with a paler pink throat, are funnel-shaped and carried in clusters on an upright plant. 'Alice' can be relied upon to flower every year and is quick to grow, making a good plant for the smaller garden.

'Arthur Bedford'.

'Arthur J. Ivens'.

'Arthur Bedford'

✿ May - mid June   U. H. 3.6 m (12 ft)
H4   F3   FCC

For those who like the unusual, the distinctively coloured flowers of this rhododendron will be very welcome. Its *ponticum* parentage shows in the pale mauve of the petals, which is offset by the very positive deep red eye in the throat. Dark green leathery leaves make a suitable background to altogether charming clusters of flowers.

'Arthur J. Ivens' ✿ April

U. H. 1.2-1.5 m (4-5 ft)   H4   F1   AM

A very pretty little rhododendron, 'Arthur J. Ivens' has as one of its parents *R. Williamsianum,* and was raised and introduced by Messrs. Hillier of Winchester in 1944. It forms a dome-shaped bush covered with more or less round-heart-shaped leaves, glaucous green. As the young shoots and leaves unfold in spring, they are tinted a reddish bronze, which blends well with the deep to pale pink, bell-shaped flowers, each marked with two small red 'flashes'.

'Augfast'
🌸 April   U. H. 90 cm (3 ft)   H4   F4

A compact, rounded little shrub, sparsely leaved. It is perfectly hardy, producing lavender-blue, funnel-shaped flowers, though there are various forms available, in which the colour can range from deep blue through to heliotrope. If a really blue-flowered one is required, this should be specified when ordering.

'Augfast'.

'Beauty of Littleworth'.

'Beauty of Littleworth'
🌸 May - early June   U. H. 6 m (20 ft)
H4   F4   FCC

This is one of the older hybrids, but still one of the best; it was raised at Littleworth in Surrey in about 1900. The magnificent white, red-spotted flowers are amongst the largest produced by any rhododendron, in equally large clusters. These, together with its height, mean that it is not suitable for a small garden, but as part of a sizable woodland garden, it will make a superb plant.

'Blue Diamond' (see p. 34).
🌸 April   U. H. 90 cm (3 ft)
H4   F4   FCC   AGM

Unlike the so-called 'blue' rose, 'Blue Diamond' really does have blue flowers. It is a small rhododendron growing slowly and is compact and rounded in habit. In April the plant apparently turns completely blue as the flowers unfold, and it is altogether singularly attractive. The rock garden, the front of a mixed border or a patio container are all good sites in which to grow it. The small, grey-green leaves have a pleasant aromatic smell when crushed.

Low growing Rhododendron 'Blue Diamond' with a young plant of Rhododendron 'Carita Golden Dream' in foreground.

'Blue Peter'.

'Blue Peter'

✿ May   U. H. 3 m (10 ft)
H4   F4   FCC   AGM

If a bold splash of blue is wanted in the garden in spring, this is the plant to provide it. Its frilly, trumpet-shaped flowers are blue, ringed with violet, paling to white in the red spotted throat. It flowers freely sometimes into June, and is strong and upright in habit.

Opposite page :
A well established border of rhododendrons and evergreen azaleas. In the foreground Rhododendron 'Blue Tit' and evergreen Azalea 'Pink Treasure', with the pale pink Rhododendron 'Temple Belle' at the back. Bracken has been used as a mulch to preserve moisture and suppress weeds.

'Bo-Peep'.

'Blue Tit' *(See page 35)*

❀ April   U. H. 90 cm (3 ft)   H4   F3

Suitable for any small garden, also useful for rock garden planting. 'Blue Tit' produces a mass of funnel shaped flowers which are borne in clusters at the end of the branches. A compact and fairly slow growing plant that flowers freely in an open position.

'Bowbells'.

'Bo-Peep'

❀ Late February - March   U. H. 1.2 m (4 ft)
H3   F4   AM

In early spring 'Bo-Peep' unfolds her primrose-yellow funnel-shaped flowers, spotted deeper yellow. Unlike many rhododendrons, the flowers come in ones or twos only, on a rather open-habited bush, with fragile shoots and branches and the whole plant has a rather delicate air; it does in fact need to have its flowers protected by planting it in a sheltered position.

'Bowbells'

❀ May   U. H. 1.6-1.8 m (5 1/2-6 ft)
H4   F4   AM

'Bowbells' has as one parent *R. Williamsianum* and this accounts for the bell-shaped flowers, which are cerise red while still buds, but unfold to a soft and charming pink. The young shoots which appear at the same time are coppery bronze, so that the whole plant is unusually colourful in spring. The rounded leaves clothe a nicely compact bush very easy to fit into a small garden, but still not out of place in a large garden as a group planting.

'Carmen'.

'Britannia'.

'Carita Inchmery'.

'Britannia'
❀ May   U. H. 1.8 m (6 ft)
H4   F4   FCC   AM

Deservedly one of the most popular hybrid rhodo-dendrons, 'Britannia' is a Dutch introduction over 50 years old. It grows slowly to form a compact, rounded plant, and is tough and wind-resistant. The glowing deep red flowers are thickly clustered against a background of distinctive pale green leaves, and are quite unlike any other rhodo-dendron in their colouring.

'Carita Inchmery'
❀ April - May   U. H. 4.5 m (15 ft)
H4   F3   AM

There are several varieties of 'Carita', this one being one of the outstanding kinds. Although a tall rhododendron, it is compact in habit, and pro-duces its biscuit-yellow rose-tinted flowers so profusely as to be covered in them down to the ground. Since it is hardy, it can be grown in a fairly open situation. Other 'Carita' forms well worth growing are 'Carita' itself, pale yellow; 'Carita Charm', pink changing to cream, and 'Carita Golden Dream', cream and pink, changing to white.

'Carmen'
❀ April-May   U. H. 0.3 m (1 ft)   H4   F4   AM

A superb dwarf rhododendron, almost prostrate in habit. The bell shaped flowers are deep waxy red appearing in spring. Carmen is ideally suited for a small garden, or rock garden. Generally not more than twelve inches when fully grown.

'Chevalier Felix de Sauvage'

✿ April-May   U. H. 3 m (10 ft)   H4   F2

Dating back to 1870, this is possibly the most reliable of the hybrids,
and the vigour of its constitution is borne out by its age. It flowers heavily every year,
however much it is ill-treated and neglected. The flowers are pure red
with a deeper red eye at the base of the flower.

'Christmas Cheer'
❀ February   U. H. 3 m (10 ft)   H4   F3

See also the cover page where a close-up shows its shape and pale pink colour in more detail. The normal flowering time for this hybrid is February, but in a mild winter, or sheltered garden, it will unfold its pink buds in January; the colour of the fully open flower is white. It was once customary to force the plant so that it flowered at Christmas, hence the name, and it is a very good plant from which to cut shoots just as the buds are unfolding and bring them into the house for extra early flowering. As with all these early kinds, the flowers are likely to be damaged by frost. A dense, compact bush, it will bloom well when still quite small, and will grow in a light or slightly shaded place.

'Cilpinense'
❀ March   U. H. 1 m (3 ft)
H4   F4   AM   AGM

This is a hybrid between two species, *R. ciliatum* and *R. moupinense,* introduced in 1927 when it immediately obtained an award. 'Cilpinense' is not very large and it is a rounded bush, on which large bell-shaped flowers are produced. The average size of the flowers is 6 cm (2 1/2 in) wide and being freely produced, make the bush startlingly attractive with the white and pink tinted petals of the open flowers and deeper pink buds mixed in with them. It flowers early, and is often caught by spring frosts, so it is best planted sheltered by a large tree or shrub.

'Cornish Cross'
✿ April-May U. H. 5 m (16 1/2 ft) H3 F4 AM

Penjerrick in Cornwall has been the home of a good many high quality
rhododendron hybrids, and this one lives up to the standard of the rest. A large, open
plant, it has inherited its peeling pinkish bark from one of its parents,
R. thomsonii. The drooping clusters of waxy, narrow bell-shaped flowers are
rosy pink when fully expanded, but in bud are deep red, so that it is
ornamental, both in bud and in full flower.

'Dairy Maid'.

Damaris Logan'.

'Dairy Maid'

❀ May   U. H. 1.8 m (6 ft)   H4   F4   AM

This is a hybrid from *R. campylocarpum,* whose flowers are pale yellow. The progeny has richly cream-coloured blooms in compact clusters, on a slow-growing, dense shrub. The throat of each flower is marked with a crimson blotch. A very attractive hybrid, but the leaves sometimes become pale, giving the plant a sickly appearance. Really well-drained soil, extra leafmould and a little nitrogenous fertilizer in spring should ensure that this does not happen.

'Damaris Logan'

❀ May   U. H. 3 m (10 ft)   H3   F3   AM

The softly yellow, funnel-shaped, rather frilly flowers of this hybrid appear in clusters of five or six; the wide open mouth of each is filled with red-tipped stamens and a red anther. As it is not quite as hardy as some, it needs a woodland setting to shelter it, and enable it to flower to perfection.

41

'Damozel'.

'Diane'.

'Damozel'

❀ May U. H. 3 m (10 ft) H 3-4 F 3 AM

'Damozel' grows fairly quickly into a spreading bush. One of its parents is *R. griersonianum,* a most striking Chinese species, and, like its parent, 'Damozel' needs a sheltered place to be at its best. The rich ruby-red flowers are spotted with black inside, and the flowering trusses are dome-shaped.

'Diane'

❀ April U. H. 3.7 m (12 ft) H 4 F 3 AM

This Dutch hybrid was introduced in 1920 and has since become one of the most popular and widely grown of the yellow rhododendrons. A compact plant, it has rather pale green leaves with a tendency to develop yellow mottling, and primrose yellow, bell-shaped flowers, marked with a red stripe inside. They appear late in April. Although the plant itself is perfectly hardy, the flowers are more delicate, prone to weather damage, so that provision of some shelter is advisable.

'Earl of Donoughmore'

❀ May U. H. 3.5 m (11 ft) H 4 F 4

In 1953 a Dutch firm of nurserymen produced a hybrid from *R. griersonianum* with large, brilliantly red flowers in clusters of 12 and more, which they called 'Earl of Donoughmore'. It grows into quite a large shrub of 3.5 m (11 ft) and more, covered in flowers in mid May, reasonably upright, provided it is planted in a sunny place. In shade it has a tendency to sprawl.

Opposite page. 'Earl of Donoughmore'

'Elizabeth Lockheart'

❀ May   U. H. 1 m (3 1/2 ft)

Whereas the flower colour of 'Elizabeth' is blood-red, that of this hybrid is most unusual, being a true beetroot-red. The colour is echoed in the new leaves and young shoots as they unfold in spring, which are also deep red.

'Elizabeth'

❀ April   U. H. 2 m (6 1/2 ft)
H4   F4   FCC   AM   AGM

'Elizabeth' is undoubtedly one of the outstanding, low-growing rhododendron hybrids. It will grow slowly to about 90 cm (3 ft) tall, reaching its ultimate height only after many years, and produces a mass of blood-red, rather waxy, trumpet-shaped flowers, each at least 7.5 cm (3 in) wide. The leaves are an unusual soft green. There is a prostrate form of this called 'Jenny' (sometimes 'Creeping Jenny'), whose flowers are longer, bigger and a lighter red. It is a little earlier flowering.

An impressive display of colour created by just three plants of the most popular Rhododendron 'Elizabeth'.

'Fabia'.

'Festival'.

'General Eisenhower'.

'Fabia'
❀ May-June   U. H. 1.8 m (6 ft)   H4   F4   AM

Prolific in flowering, 'Fabia' has a rather squat habit, spreading rather than upright. In early summer, trusses of funnel-shaped orange to salmon flowers unfold, backed by greyish green leaves of exactly the right tone to set off the orange flowers to perfection. Completely hardy, it is a first-class plant for any garden, especially as it extends the flowering season.

'Festival'
❀ May   U. H. 3.4 m (11 ft)

Strong carmine-red flowers with a rather waxy appearance which are held well above the foliage. The narrow leaves have an unusual and attractive ribbed effect. The rhododendron when fully grown forms a round, spreading bush.

'General Eisenhower'
❀ May - early June   U. H. 1.5 m (5 ft)   H4   F1

One of the parents of this hybrid is *R. griffithianum,* a really magnificent rhododendron from Sikkim. The hybrid itself is small for rhododendrons, being as wide as it is tall when fully grown. It becomes covered in scarlet, frilly blossoms and is a good plant for the smaller garden, with a strong constitution.

'Goldsworth Yellow'

✿ April - early May   U. H. 5 m (17 ft)
H4   F3   AM

This is one of the most popular and oldest
of the yellow hybrid rhododendrons. It has
been grown since at least 1913, and even after
being propagated for so long, remains a strong
and hardy plant, flowering at the end of April
or in early May. The more or less funnel-shaped
flowers are apricot coloured in bud, but open
to pale yellow, speckled brown in the throat.
There may be as many as 16 in a cluster.
The bush is dome-shaped, eventually to about
5 m (17 ft) tall, and will grow well in sun, as
well as shade.

'Hardize's Beauty'

✿ May   U. H. 1 m (3 ft)   H4   F3

The Dutch have contributed a great deal to
horticulture and to rhododendron and azalea
hybridization in particular; this is an unusual
hybrid of Dutch breeding from a cross between
R. racemosum and a pink Japanese azalea.
It is hardly surprising that the flowers are clear
pink, since both parents have flowers of that
colour, and in spring the plant will be covered
in them. For the rest of the year it will be
neatly clothed in small, glossy leaves tinted
purple.

'Harvest Moon'

✿ May   U. H. 1.8-2.1 m (6-7 ft)
H4   F3   AM

The names of plants often give no clue as to
the appearance of the plant, but this one is
well-named since the flowers are a beautiful
creamy colour. They are bell-shaped, and
the inside of each is marked in the throat
with a crimson blotch. The plant is slow-
growing, to about 90 cm (3 ft) after ten years
and eventually will reach its ultimate height
with a width of about 1.5 m (5 ft). It has a
compact habit.

'Hawk Crest'

✿ May   U. H. 3.6-4.5 m (12-15 ft)
H3   F3   FCC

One of the most outstanding rhododendrons,
though still fairly scarce. However, it is very
well worth growing and will do more than do
justice to a lightly wooded position. It is one
of Lionel de Rothschild's hybrids from his
garden at Exbury, first flowered in 1950. The
buds are deep orange, changing to lemon-
yellow as they unfold, and each flower truss
contains about a dozen flowers, held erect.
The result is a magnificent spectacle. 'Hawk
Crest' forms a rather open, loose plant.

'Hollandia'.

'Humming Bird'.

'Hollandia'

✿ May   U. H. 3.6 m (12 ft)   H 4   F 2

'Hollandia' has as one parent the hybrid 'Pink Pearl', but, although the latter is lilac-pink to white with crimson markings, 'Hollandia is carmine-red.

'Humming Bird'

✿ April-May   U. H. 1.8 m (6 ft)   H 3   F.

A delightful *williamsianum* hybrid, one of the best raised. Its *haemotodes* ("blood-like" parentage gives it the beautiful deep red waxy, bell-shaped flowers on a small dome shaped bush with somewhat rounded leaves Hardy in most parts of the country, roon should be made for it whether the garden i large or small.

'Ivery's Scarlet'

❀ May   U. H. 3-4 m (10-12 ft)   H 4   F 3

While rhododendrons can be exceedingly good 'specimen' plants grown alone, perhaps at one end of a lawn or as a focal point to a garden entrance, they will also combine happily with their own kind or with other shrubs. Here, a scarlet-flowered and a pink-flowered hybrid form a colourful association when they flower in late spring; the red of 'Ivery's Scarlet' is sufficiently modified by the green foliage to prevent any suggestion of 'killing' the pink of 'Astarte'. *(See page 50)*.

'Lady Rosebery'.

'Lady Bessborough Montreal'.

'Lady Rosebery'

❀ May   U. H. 4.5 m (15 ft)
H 3   F 3   FCC   AM

The rhododendron genus is so large that it has been divided up into what are known as Series by the botanists, each Series having some characteristic which differentiates it from the others. The Series which has *R. cinnabarinum* in it has tubular, waxy, flowers in shades of orange, quite unlike the form generally considered to be typical of rhododendron flowers. 'Lady Rosebery' is a hybrid from this species, with the most lovely pinky orange blooms. The blue-grey leaves tone satisfyingly with the flowers, on quite a tall plant, woodland conditions suit it best.

'Lady Bessborough Montreal'

❀ End May - early June   U. H. 3 m (10 ft)
H 4   F 4

This form of 'Lady Bessborough' is late flowering, and its buds are pink, but they change to deep cream or biscuit colour as they unfold. It is remarkably profuse flowering.

Loderi'
❀ Late April-May   U. H. 5 m (16 ft)   H 3   F 3-4

The most famous hybrid of them all is a cross between the species *fortunei* and *griffithianum,*
raised by Sir Edmund Loder in 1901. Apart from its spectacular and enormous clusters of trumpet-shaped fragrant,
white to pink flowers, up to 15 cm (6 in) wide, it also has extremely handsome
grey-green foliage. The young leaves are particularly attractive when unfolding in early spring.
The plant becomes a large shrub or small tree in time.

'Loderi Astarte'
❀ May   U. H. 5 m (16 1/2 ft)   H 3   F 3-4

As with all this group, this is a superb plant, whose magnificent, large soft pink flowers are exquisitely scented.
The leaves are a very distinctive grey-green, typical of a 'Loderi' plant.

Yellow Rhododendron 'Dairymaid',
Ivery's Scarlet' *and* 'Loderi Astarte' *adding colour to a woodland path.*

'Loderi King George'

⚛ May   U. H. 5.5 m (17 1/2 ft)   H3   F3-4   FCC   AM   AGM

The hybrid 'Loderi' is considered to be the most outstanding one ever produced.
The trusses of flowers on its form 'King George' are enormous, and the funnel-shaped flowers
are pink in bud, unfolding to white with green marking in the base
of the throat. This is the best form, which certainly lives up to its imperial name.

Rhododendron 'Loder's White' *and* 'Pilgrim' *in a woodland border.*

'Madame Masson'.

'Loder's White'
❀ May U. H. 5 m (17 ft)
H3 F4 AM AGM

'Pilgrim'
❀ May U. H. 5 m (17 ft) H4 F4 AM

'Loder's White' is still the most widely planted of all the white rhododendrons, after being in existence for nearly a hundred years. It is thought by some to be the best hardy hybrid rhododendron ever produced. The enormous, conically-shaped flowers, at least 10 cm (4 in) wide, are deceptive in that the buds are pink; it is not until they open that they turn white, when they are thinly spotted with crimson. 'Loder's White' grows to about 5 m (17 ft). 'Pilgrim', also a tall-growing plant, has superb clusters of large, trumpet-shaped flowers, coloured deep pink. Both hybrids flower in May.

'Madame Masson'
❀ May U. H. 4.8 m (16 ft) H4 F1

'Madame Masson' is a very old hybrid, first being flowered in 1849. It is extremely hardy, inheriting this quality from its parents *R. ponticum,* and *R. catawbiense* a native of North Carolina in America, where it has been found to survive 60 degrees of frost. 'Madame Masson' forms a first-class evergreen hedge, with the added attraction of flowers — white with a yellow blotch — or it can be used as a screen.

'Manon'
✿ May   U. H. 3.4 m (11 ft)

A cross from the popular rhododendron 'Sappho', the large white flowers are held well above the foliage and have a distinctive deep purple flash in the throat. This variety has a rather open habit of growth.

'Marie Martine'
✿ June   U. H. 3.4 m (11 ft)

A useful hybrid to prolong the flowering season in to June. The pale pink buds open to white flowers with frilled edges and attractive yellow markings in the throat. This is a useful plant to place among some of the stronger reds and pinks.

Manon'.

'Marie Martine'.

'May Day'.

'Moerheim Pink'.

'May Day'
❀ May - early June   U. H. 2 m (6 1/2 ft)
H 3   F 4   AM   AGM

This is another hybrid which should be better known than it is; it is late flowering, producing startlingly brilliant red, wax-like flowers, backed by grey-blue leaves apparently sprinkled with white powder. 'May Day' really is outstanding, and does not grow large, though somewhat spreading.

'Moerheim Pink'
❀ April-May   U. H. 2.2 m (7 ft)   H 4   F 4

From Europe, this hardy and compact hybrid has large, open clear pink, bell-like flowers in great profusion. The rounded leaves suggest that its parentage has *orbiculare* or *williamsianum* in it; eventual height is about 2.2 m (7 ft), but in ten years it may only reach 1 m (3 1/2 ft). It is an excellent substitute for 'Pink Pearl' in a small garden.

'Moonshine Supreme'

✿ April   U. H. 5 m (15 ft)   H4   F4

In 1953 the Royal Horticultural Society of England flowered this hybrid at the Wisley Garden in Surrey, and it has subsequently proved to be both hardy and beautiful. The compact trusses consist of wide-open, rather flat flowers, primrose-yellow in colour. With the popularity that yellow rhododendrons have, it is surprising that it is not more widely known.

'Moonstone'

✿ April - early May   U. H. 1.5 m (5 ft)
H3   F4

This is rather a rainbow of a plant; its rounded, bright green leaves are attractive at any time, and they are enhanced by the delicate creamy yellow, bell-shaped, nodding flowers, edged with pink, which unfold from brown-red buds. The plant is dome-shaped, and not tall, and it would be a decided asset to any garden.

'Moser's Maroon'.

'Moser's Maroon
❀ May   U. H. 4.5 m (15 ft)   H4   F4   AM

One of the criticisms made of rhododendrons is that they have one glorious burst of colour in late spring, and then subside into mediocrity for the rest of the year. 'Moser's Maroon', a French hybrid, escapes this castigation, however, as it has bright distinctive red bark on all the new growth, and the young leaves are fiery copper-red, only fading in autumn. The deep maroon-red flowers, black-spotted, provide a striking combination with the young growth thoughout May, and the total effect is quite remarkable. Tall and vigorous, the plant will grow moderately quickly to its ultimate height.

Hostas associated with 'Mrs G. W. Leak'.

Ground-cover plants help to fill in gaps in rhododendron plantings, and can provide ornament at other times of the year than spring, as these hostas do, both with their handsome leaves, and lily-like flowers in summer. The rhododendron hybrid associated with them is 'Mrs G. W. Leak'.

'Mrs Furnival'

❀ May - early June   U. H. 1.8 - 2.4 m (6-8 ft)   H4   F4   FCC   AGM

A famous hybrid of 1920 vintage, 'Mrs Furnival' is a slow growing plant of
a few inches a year once established. Habit is compact and surprisingly dense. The flowers
are softly pink, funnel-shaped, blotched with wine in the throat,
and gathered in tightly packed trusses. This is a well-tried and reliable plant
which would not overwhelm a small garden.

'Mrs G. W. Leak'

❀ May - early June   U. H. 4.5 m (15 ft)   H4   F4   FCC   AGM

Unusually coloured flowers make this Dutch hybrid rhododendron stand out
amongst the crowd; they are large and open-funnel-shaped, rosy pink and with a conspicuous
black to dark brown blotch in the throat which catches the eye at once.

'Mrs Furnival'.

'Naomi Exbury'

❀ May   U. H. 4.5-5 m (15-17 ft)   H4   F3

That famous Rothschild garden at Exbury
has been the nursery of very many first-class
rhododendron hybrids, and 'Naomi Exbury'
is one of the best, being a form of 'Naomi',
itself a wonderful rhododendron. It is quite
large, clothed in grey-green leaves, which give it
a curiously clean-cut appearance. Large, fragrant, wide open flowers in pastel shades of
lilac-pink, tinted pale yellow, unfold from
cerise-crimson buds.

'Naomi Glow'

❀ April   U. H. 4.5 m (15 ft)   H4   F3-4

Unusually for rhododendrons, this is a hybrid
with fragrant flowers, large and wide open,
sparkling pink, with brown markings in the
throat. It is an extremely attractive Exbury
hybrid, with an open habit. The leaves are
more grey than green and, besides being just the
right foil for the flowers, ensure that the plant is
more ornamental out of flower than most of the
rhododendrons.

'Pierre Moser'

❀ Late Feb.-March   U. H. 3 m (15-17 ft)
H4   F1

Since the flower quality has only been given
a rating of 1, it will be realised that this hybrid
needs a protected site which will always be free
of spring frost, otherwise the flowers will be
ruined.. Flowering is early, sometimes in late
February, but more usually in March, and
the plant has the added merit of beginning
to flower when very young. Large, rounded
pink blooms come on a tidily-shaped plant.

'Pink Pearl'

❀ April - early May   U. H. 5 m (16 1/2 ft)
H4   F4   AM   AGM

'Pink Pearl' is a hybrid rhododendron which
has caught the public fancy so that it is probably
found in more gardens than any other hybrid.
It is undoubtedly very pretty when in bloom,
with its large, delicately lilac-to-pink flowers
fading to white at the edges, but it has a
tendency to become rather bare and gaunt at its
foot. It is strong and fairly fast growing
and would be happiest in woodland. As it ages,
groundcover plants round it, for instance
species cyclamen, erythroniums and *Cornus
canadensis,* would help to overcome the
ugliness of the sparse growth lower down.

'Praecox'.

'Purple Splendour'.

'Princess Anne'.

'Praecox'

❀ Feb.-March   U. H. 2 m (6 1/2 ft)
H 4   F 4   AGM

A 'must' for every garden, and it is in fact very popular, as it has the merits of being not only extremely pretty, but early flowering and small. Funnel-shaped, translucent, rosy lilac flowers open on a plant no more than 2 m (6 1/2 ft) after many years. A sheltered position, to protect the flowers from frost, is advisable.

'Princess Anne'

❀ Late April   U. H. 70 cm (2 1/2 ft)   H 4   F 4

A really charming new dwarf hybrid rhododendron ideally suited to any small garden. It forms a dense low growing shrub, which is covered in a mass of pale yellow flowers during April and May. Unfortunately at the moment this plant is in short supply.

'Purple Splendour'

❀ May-June   U. H. 2 m (6 1/2 ft)
H 4   F 4   AM

Amongst the pinks, reds, oranges and yellows which commonly occur in rhododendron hybrids, a true purple is unusual, but this one has the genuine imperial purple for its flower colour, emphasized with a prominent black ray in the throat. As well as this, it flowers profusely, rather late, particularly if grown under a light covering of trees. Its upright habit is reminiscent of one of its parents, *R. ponticum*. Its medium height makes it a good plant for the smaller garden.

'President Roosevelt'

✿ May   U. H. 3-4 m (10-12 ft)

It is very much a mystery as to why this hybrid is not more popular and better known.
The combination of really exciting foliage, ideal for flower arranging,
and beautiful flowers, must be unique and yet, in spite of being
cultivated for many years, this Belgian hybrid has never gained the popularity which is
so well deserved. The dark green leaves are splashed with gold in various shades,
and the equally beautiful flowers are white, shading to pale pink and
finally to red at the frilled edges, like a picotee carnation. To get the most marked
variegation, this hybrid should be planted in the open, not in the shade.

'Quaver'.

'Remo'.

'Quaver'

✿ March-April   U. H. 1.5 m (5 ft)   H 4   F 2

The parents of this charming little hybrid are *R. leucaspis* and *R. sulfureum;* both are small, with a tendency to early flowering. In a mild spring, the first clusters of pale yellow flowers will appear but, sadly, it is not completely hardy, and it should only be planted in warm sheltered gardens. Otherwise not only will the flowers be browned by frost, but the plant itself may be checked or even killed.

'Remo'

✿ April   U. H. 1.5 m (5 ft)   H 3   F 3

A small, yellow-flowered shrub sums up this hybrid; it is in fact semi-dwarfing, growing slowly to its maximum height and whose clear, bright yellow, open flowers appear early. A little shelter will ensure that they are not spoilt by spring air-frosts.

'Rotenburg' *(foliage)*.

'Rotenburg'.

'Sapphire'.

'Rotenburg'

✿ April-May   U. H. 3-4 m (10-12 ft)

Large, creamy-white, funnel-shaped flowers are produced on this plant; they are beautiful in their own right, but the foliage is just as exciting, being bright apple-green and glossy all the year. In spring, the new leaves unfold to reveal surfaces so brightly shining and polished as almost to have been painted with clear varnish.

'Sapphire'

✿ April   U. H. 45 cm (1 1/2 ft)
H4   F4   AM

This is a good little plant for the rock garden, covering itself in open funnels of lavender-blue, centred with a mass of long delicate stamens. Its width is equal to its height. The small grey-green leaves are barely visible at flowering time, but make the plant an attractive hummock at other times.

'Sappho'
✿ Late May   U. H. 4.5 m (15 ft)
H4   F3   AM   AGM

A rhododendron hybrid with quite startlin
flowers, as they are pure white, with a pronoun
ced rich purple blotch in the throat, overlai
with black. In dome-shaped clusters of fiftee
or more, 7 cm (3 in) wide, funnel-shaped flower
appear in late May or early June. An ol
hybrid introduced by Waterer's before 1867
'Sappho' will grow to about 4.5 m (15 ft)
with a tendency to spread. Pruning is usuall
necessary when mature to contain it an
maintain flowering.

'Souvenir de Dr S. Endtz
✿ Late April-May   U. H. 3.6 m (12 ft)
H4   F3   FCC   AM   AGM

The well known and very popular 'Pink Pear
is one of this hybrid's parents, and it could i
fact be described as a rosy red form of 'Pin
Pearl'. The large funnel-shaped flowers ar
the same shape and open in similarly dome
shaped trusses. It originated in Boskoop, i
Holland, early in this century.

'Sappho'.

'Souvenir de Dr S. Endtz'

'Songbird'
✿ April - early May   U. H. 1.5 m (5 ft)
H4   F4   AM

Like 'Sapphire' this has 'Blue Tit' as one c
its parents, giving it the deep violet colour c
its bell-shaped flowers. It is a Scottish hybri
raised by Col. Sir James Horlick in 195
and is comparatively modern.

'Songbird'

'Seven Stars'

❀ May - mid June   U. H. 4.5 m (16 1/2 ft)
H3   F4   AM

'Seven Stars' is a comparatively new hybrid, raised at
Windsor Great Park, whose award was given in 1967, and
which has a potentially very good future, though it is
still rather difficult to obtain. Vigorous and strong
growing, it flowers freely and reliably, with bell-shaped
blooms, white with a pink flush, and frilly edged. The
buds are red to deep pink.

'Souvenir of W. C. Slocock'

❀ May - early June   U. H. 3 m (10 ft)   H4   F4   AM

The Slocock nursery is one of those in Britain specia-
lising in growing and breeding rhododendrons, and this
hybrid, named after one of the family, is a first-class
plant, vigorous and densely habited, with a medium
height when fully grown. In early summer, its pale
orange-pink buds unfold to exquisitely softly coloured
pale yellow, flushed apricot and pink, bell-shaped flowers.
Completely hardy, it is a choice plant for any garden.

'Seven Stars'.

'Souvenir of W. C. Slocock'.

65

'Susan'

✿ April-May   U. H. 3.6 m (12 ft)   H4   F4   FCC   AM   AGM

There is a herbaceous perennial commonly called Black-eyed Susan, which has
yellow flowers with a black centre, and it happens that this hybrid rhododendron has lavender
coloured flowers, with a conspicuous, much deeper lavender eye.
The edges of the petals are also darker. The rounded leaves cover a tall, bushy plant,
and although flowering time can be April in an early season, early May is more normal.
The contrasting colours of these two rhododendrons, the soft lavender-blue of 'Susan' and the pale
pink-and-white butterfly-like flowers of *yunnanense* are
an example of happy blending of the right tones in flower colour, when a straightforward
hard mauve and a bright rose-pink would have been too crude, and too hard on the eye.
As it is, these two form a charming picture in late April and May.
'Susan' is moderately tall, to about 3.6 m (12 ft); height of *yunnanense* is a little less, 3 m (10 ft).

'Unique'

✿ April U. H. 1.8 m (6 ft) H4 F3 FCC AM

It can be safely said that the name of this hybrid is also appropriate since in no other plant will the flower colour be found. Described variously as biscuit-yellow, ochre flushed apricot, creamy white tinted pink, ochre tinged peach or flesh changing to buff, the colour is not only unique but seems to defy accurate description. The bush on which these distinctive flowers are found is compact and very handsome.

'Temple Belle'

✿ April U. H. 1.5 m (5 ft) H3 F3

It would be difficult to find a more appropriate name for this plant; it comes from China, it is exceptionally pretty and the flower shape could be described in no other way. The pale rose-pink bell flowers hang downwards in clusters of three or four on a plant. Heart-shaped and rounded, the grey-green leaves cover a mound-shaped plant to ground level, making it attractive all the year. The shelter of light woodland will enable it to grow to perfection.

'Unique'.

'Temple Belle'.

'Val d'Aulnay'

❀ May   U. H. 3.4 m (11 ft)

Large trusses of clear pink flowers edged with salmon appear in early May.
The plant has a neat round habit.

Two hybrids of R. ponticum in the garden of Le Vastérival, 'Purple Splendour' has the deep purple flowers.

R. luteum gives a brilliant display of yellow, fragrant flowers on the left side of this woodland path in the garden of Le Vastérival.

New growth on large-leaved rhododendrons

The new shoots and leaves of the large-leaved rhododendrons are handsome in their own right as they
unfold, with the paler green underside to the leaves
and the reddish scales which enclose the buds. When
fully expanded, the leaves of many of these rhododendrons have a rust-brown indumentum on the underside. Flowers and leaves thus combine to produce
magnificent plants. As they are trees rather than
shrubs, they must have plenty of space and, preferably,
lightly wooded surroundings.

Leaf detail on rhododendron species

This illustration gives an idea of the tremendous
variation in size and shape of the leaves of the different
rhododendrons. It is difficult to believe that they may
be only 1.3 cm (1/2 in) long in the shrublets, yet more
than 30 cm (1 ft) in such giants as *R. macabeanum*. All
sorts of shades of green : light green, olive green, blue
and grey-green, as well as rust and reddish brown
indumentum on the undersides, can be seen, and the
shape will be just as varied, from round and heart-like
to narrow and rolled over, almost needle-like. Their
leaves alone would qualify rhododendrons for a place
in any garden.

Rhododendron species

There can be few gardens in Northern Europe, particularly Britain, that do not have a rhododendron
in them somewhere, whether it is a species, a hybrid, or one of the many azaleas. The genus is a large one, containing
more than 500 species, found in the mostly mountainous forest of the Himalayas,
China and Tibet, and great numbers of new species were discovered and sent back by plant hunters in the
early 1900s. The species are easily as attractive as the specially bred hybrids,
and the list which follows includes some of the choicest; it also shows the tremendous
range of colour and of size, from tiny shrublets for the rock garden, to the 9 m (30 ft) trees for woodland.
All the colours of the rainbow, including green, are found in the flowers of the genus. Rhododendrons are almost
always evergreen, though there are one or two which are deciduous or semi-deciduous.
There is also a group of azaleas which is deciduous.

Rhododendron 'Augustinii' forming a mass of blue flowers. In the foreground is Azalea 'Iro-hayama'.

R. bureavii.

R. augustinii
✿ May   U. H. 4.5 m (15 ft)   H 3-4   F 2-4

Augustine Henry was a Medical Officer in the Chinese customs during the last fifty years of the 19th century, and this species, which commemorates him, is the nearest to true blue of all the rhododendron species. It flowers exceedingly freely, the blooms being funnel-shaped, on a quickly growing plant. Plants growing in the wild have been found to vary considerably in colour, from rose-pink to deep violet, and the forms available in cultivation may also be very different in their shades of blue and violet-blue. It has been found, too, that the flower colour on one plant can be different from year to year. A lightly shaded place is the most suitable, though it will still grow well in the open.

R. catawbiense 'Grandiflorum Album'.

R. bureavii
✿ April-May   U. H. 2.4 m (8 ft)   H 4   F 3

This Chinese rhododendron grows high up in Yunnan, China at an altitude of 3,900 m (13,000 ft). It has rose-pink, bell-shaped flowers, marked with crimson. However, it has another attraction in the foliage, which has a thick, bright rusty red felt, or indumentum, on the undersurface, very attractive in winter sunshine. The stems of the young growths also have a coat of this woolly felt, varying from pale fawn to bright rust in colour.

R. catawbiense 'Grandiflorum Album'
✿ May - early June   U. H. 4.5 m (15 ft)
H 4   F 2

The albino or white-flowered form of the Catawba rhododendron. It flowers profusely and is especially good as an informal hedge, or screen. Many shrubs make good flowering hedges, if grown informally so that their flowers are allowed to remain and are not clipped off with the annual close trim of a formal hedge.

R. catawbiense 'Grandiflorum'

✿ May - early June   U. H. 4.5 m (15 ft)   H 4   F 1

The Catawba river in North Carolina is the origin of the name of this species.
Its chief merit is that of extreme hardiness, which makes it tolerant of even the sub-zero
temperatures of Scandinavia, and it is therefore a popular
garden plant throughout Northern Europe. In Britain it is less often grown, perhaps
because it is like the much-naturalized *ponticum,* with its lilac-purple flowers
in May and early June. In time, it will grow into a large shrub about 4.5 m (15 ft) tall.

R. davidsonianum
❀ Late April-May   U. H. 3 m (10 ft)
H 3-4   F 2-4   FCC   AM   AGM

A Chinese rhododendron, sent back by the plant collector, E. H. Wilson, in 1908, this species has a rather open habit. Its unusually narrow, dark green leaves are the backing for flowers which vary considerably in colour from form to form. Purplish-rose, pink, pale rose or white, and shades in between may occur, and the flowers may also be marked with reddish spots. One of the best pink forms has received an AM, and these pink-flowered kinds are the ones to order. All are completely hardy.

R. impeditum
❀ April - early May   U. H. A few cm (in)
H4   F 3-4   AM   AGM

The variation in size amongst rhododendrons is enormous, but not generally appreciated: they can vary from tiny creeping shrublets to trees of 9 m (30 ft) and more tall. This is one of the smallest, only a few cm (in) high, consisting of a tangle of branchlets clothed in tiny blue-green leaves less than 2 cm (1 in) long and equally small mauve or purplish blue open flowers covering the plant. It comes from high up in the mountains of Yunnan, China and should have the most exposed position possible, preferably on a rock garden.

R. 'Lutescens'

✿ February-April   U. H. 3-4 m (10-12 ft)
H3   F3   FCC   AGM

A beautiful early-flowering rhododendron. New growth in the spring is an attractive bronzy-red colour, also the foliage gives another excellent show of colour in the autumn. The delicate, pale yellow flowers, with elegant long stamens appear at any time from February-April, covering the whole bush in a mass of flowers. Being an early flowering rhododendron, *R.* 'Lutescens' requires a sheltered position.

R. mucronulatum

✿ January-March   U. H. 2.7 m (8 ft)
H4   F3   AM   AGM

Winter flowers are always welcome, and the blooms of this rhododendron species appear in the first week of the New Year. They are completely frost resistant and are a bright rosy purple, funnel shape. Most unusually for rhododendrons, it is deciduous. Occasionally the new growth is damaged by frost, but the plant repairs this later in the season. Planted with the golden-flowered witch-hazel, *Hamamelis mollis,* the winter garden will be immeasurably cheered.

R. oreotrephes
❀ April-May   U. H. 6 m (20 ft)
H4   F2   AM

The Tibetan and Burmese mountains are the home of this rhododendron species, which forms a large shrub. It flowers profusely and varies a great deal from form to form in the colour of its flowers, which range from pale mauve with brownish crimson spots through shades of lavender-pink to deep rosy lilac. The leaves also vary in shape from long to round, and have an attractive bloom on them; in cold gardens it loses its foliage in winter, but even so, is very well worth growing as it is highly ornamental.

R. ponticum 'Variegatum'
❀ May-June   U. H. 6 m (20 ft)   H4   F1

The wild rhododendron in its plain-leaved form can be seen growing in woodlands and similar sites all over the British Isles. It is much used as a hedge, and has purple flowers in May and June. The variety, whose leaves are irregularly marked in creamy-white on the margins, is much less vigorous and invasive, and its flowers are a pale lavender. It is especially popular with flower arranging enthusiasts. Height can eventually be about 6 m (20 ft), but it can be contained without harm as a much smaller plant.

R. ponticum

✿ May-June   U. H. 3.6-6 m (10-20 ft)

Ponticum has become naturalized to such an extent in Britain that it is often regarded as a native plant, even a weed. However, the name is taken from that of a town in Asia Minor, Pontus, and it does in fact grow wild in Asia Minor, the Caucasus, Spain, Portugal and Armenia.

It was introduced to Britain from Gibraltar in 1763 and, the British climate being ideal for it, *ponticum* has now become one of the most distinctive of evergreen shrubs in the landscape.

Formal hedges of *ponticum* are dense and evergreen, and withstand regular clipping with equanimity; it is excellent as a shelter belt and grows to between 3.6 m (10 and 20 ft).

As a flowering shrub, it is also uncommonly attractive; depending on the clone, the flowers can vary in colour from pale lilac-pink to mauve, and appear in May and June.

The banks of these shrubs naturalized in many woodlands present a splendid spectacle at this time, and this species should not be dismissed, simply because it is so easily grown. Informal hedges allowed to flower and not clipped closely, are especially attractive.

R. quinquefolium.

R. racemosum.

R. sinogrande.

R. quinquefolium
🌼 April-May   U. H. 7.5 m (25 ft)   H4   F2   AM

This azalea species is quite a large, twiggy shrub or a small tree, which can be difficult to establish, and needs cosseting in its youth. Its delicate, startlingly pure white bells, green spotted and 5 cm (2 in) wide are well worth the trouble; the young leaves are also attractive with an edging of red-brown in spring, and again later in autumn when they change to orange and red.

R. racemosum
🌼 April   U. H. Extremely variable
H4   F3   FCC   AGM

Racemosum is one of the best of the smaller species rhododendrons and more than deserves its Award of Garden Merit. It is easily grown from seed, and height varies a good deal from a few inches to 1.8 m (6 ft). Flower colour also varies, from rose pink to pale pink, or even white. It has the habit, unusual in rhododendrons, of flowering all along the stems, instead of at the shoot tips only. This, together with its elegant grey-green leaves, make it a particularly pretty plant. Flowering time is generally April. A planting with heathers produces one of the happier blends of plants in the garden.

R. sinogrande
🌼 April   U. H. 9 m (30 ft)

In 1912, the famous plant collector, George Forrest was staggered to come across a rhododendron species growing in the forests of Burma and Tibet which had leaves 90 cm (3 ft) long, and 30 cm (1 ft) wide. The altitude at which he found these plants was 3,000 - 4,200 m (10-14,000 ft), where they varied between being large shrubs or trees 9 m (30 ft) and more tall. With shelter from wind and plenty of moisture, they are magnificent plants for the large garden or woodland. The flower trusses are large, containing at least twenty flowers, bell-shaped and creamy white with a crimson blotch in the throat. There is a northern form which has softly yellow flowers. Out of flower, the leaves will always be a talking point, especially as they have a silvery-grey, or biscuit-coloured indumentum on the undersurface.

R. williamsianum
🌼 April   U. H. 1.5 m (5 ft)   H3-4   F2-3

This Chinese species is undoubtedly one of the 'top ten' of rhododendrons. Although it needs the shelter of light woodland, or an enclosed garden, this condition is not difficult to provide in one part of the garden or another. A neat mounded shrub, it is clothed with rounded grey-green leaves, tinted bronze when young. In spring, the plant unfolds single clear pink bells which last all through April. There is a form whose flowers are pink in bud but as they open fully, they turn white. This is another surprise for those who only know the rhododendrons as having funnel-shaped flowers and long rather narrow, dark green leaves. Pretty all the year round, this species is really charming in spring.

R. williamsianum.

R. yakushimanum
❀ May   U. H. 1.2 m (4 ft)   H4   F4   AGM   FCC

This species is the most outstanding of all semi-dwarf rhododendrons, and should be included in all gardens, large or small, that can grow the ericaceous plants. Found growing wild only on the island of Yakushima, off Japan, this magnificent rhododendron was introduced in 1934. A dome-shaped height of 1.2 m (4 ft) is reached only slowly, and mostly it is seen as a low-growing, spreading shrub, with dark green narrow leaves, setting off flowers starkly white when they open, though deep pink in bud. When in flower towards the end of May, the whole plant can be completely covered with blossom. The new leaves in spring have a silvery covering, and the undersides of all have a velvety brown indumentum. Altogether *yakushimanum* is a really beautiful rhododendron throughout the year.

R. yakushimanum.

R. yunnanense

※ May   U. H. 3.6 m (12 ft)   H4   F2-4   AM   AGM

Ideal for woodland planting, this appealing rhododendron species appears
to be covered in a mass of delicate pink or mauve butterflies all through May.
The flower colour can vary a great deal from form to form,
and may be white, pale pink, rose pink, rose-lavender or lavender.
It has the pleasing ability to grow in sun or shade, though a little shade is preferred.

Deciduous azaleas

The azaleas are a type of rhododendron and are referred to botanically as rhododendron
according to the species, e.g. R. luteum, R. japonica and so on. The species, like rhododendrons proper,
have been much crossed and selected to produce a vast group of very beautiful flowering shrubs,
the flowers of some being double or 'hose-in-hose'.
They include the Knap Hill Hybrids, which were originally produced in the nursery of that name in Surrey,
England. These are characterised by their trumpet-shaped, May-flowering blooms,
without fragrance, and with a considerable range of colour. Height is about 1.8-2.5 m (6-8 ft).
The Ghent Hybrids come from Belgium and have scented, honeysuckle-shaped flowers with a mass of long
stamens emerging from the tube. They flower at the end of May.
The Mollis azaleas are crossed with R. japonicum (syn. R. molle) and have large,
scentless flowers on bare branches in early May; plants are 1.2-1.8 m (4-6 ft) tall.
These are the main groups; two others are the Occidentale Hybrids, fragrant and late-May flowering, and the
Rustica Hybrids, all of medium height, with double, fragrant flowers in late May.

A magnificent display of deciduous azaleas at Exbury Gardens.

'Berryrose'

⚘ May   U. H. 2 m (6 1/2 ft)   H4   F3   AM

This is a Knap Hill Hybrid, one of the best deciduous kinds, whose rose-pink flowers have a distinctive yellow blotch. The young leaves and shoots are coppery green in colour.

'Coccinea Speciosa'

⚘ End May   U. H. 1.5 m (5 ft)
H4   F4   AGM

One of the really old hybrid azaleas, introduced before 1846, from Holland, this was finally given its award in 1969. As a Ghent Hybrid it flowers late covering itself with a mass of what can only be described as brilliant orange-red flowers which make up in quantity for their smallish size. Height is about 1.5 m (5 ft) but spread is more, to 2.1 m (7 ft).

'Berryrose'.

'Coccinea Speciosa'.

'Farall Yellow'

✿ May   U. H. 1.5 m (5 ft)   H 4   F 4   AM

Unlike another azalea in this group of the same colour, 'Klondyke', this azalea has flowers which are clear yellow, both in bud and when they unfold — there is no hint of red flushing at any time. A Knap Hill Hybrid, its funnel-shaped flowers will last for several weeks.

'Fireball'

✿ May   U. H. 2 m (6.5 ft)   H 4   F 4

Brilliant, fiery-orange red flowers contrasting with a deep red foliage, this is a really beautiful Knap Hill azalea.

'Fireglow'

✤ May U. H. 2 m (6 1/2 ft) H 4 F 4

One of the Knap Hill Hybrids, this is an azalea whose orange-vermillion flowers completely justify its name. Final height, which is rather slowly reached, is about 2 m (6 1/2 ft). The fragrant flowers appear in May.

'Gibraltar'

✤ May U. H. 2 m (6.5 ft) H 4 F 4

One of the best known of the deciduous azaleas. The buds are an attractive crimson-orange opening to large flame-orange flowers with slightly frilled petals.

'Harvest Moon'
⚜ May   U. H. 2 m (6 1/2 ft)   H4   F4   AM

The clear yellow blooms of this Knap Hill Hybrid have a pronounced deeper yellow flare in the throat, and a well-grown plant in May is quite outstanding. It is not, however, a strong grower and needs careful positioning and feeding.

'Homebush'
⚜ End May   U. H. 2 m (6 1/2 ft)
H4   F4   AM   AGM

The almost-completely round heads of flowers distinguish this Knap Hill raised azalea from all others; the colour of the partly double flowers is deep carmine red, shading out to pale rose pink.

'Hotspur'.

'Klondyke'.

R. japonicum.

'Hotspur'
✿ May   U. H. 2 m (6 1/2 ft)   H4   F4   AM

An extremely popular azalea from the Knap Hill stable, the flame-red and yellow flowers are about 10 cm (4 in) wide at their fullest extent; the upper petals have dark brown markings on the inside.

R. japonicum
(syn. *R. molle* or *Azalea mollis*)

✿ May   U. H. 3 m (10 ft)   H4   F3-4

While the azaleas are renowned mainly for their glorious flower colours, some of the deciduous kinds are also highly decorative in autumn when their leaves change colour before falling. *Azalea mollis,* as it used to be called, is one of these, as can be seen from the picture; in May the funnel-shaped, orange-red flowers unfold before the leaves. *R. japonicum* has been used a great deal as a parent plant for the many azalea hybrids now available.

'Klondyke'
✿ May   U. H. 2 m (6 1/2 ft)   H4   F3

The golden-yellow of the flowers of this Knap Hill Hybrid make an outstanding plant in any garden, and it is one of the best hybrids in its group. The flowers are large, flushed red on the reverse and also red when in bud, offset by coppery-red leaves and shoots.

Primulas, white trilliums, blue Tibetan poppies and the round leaves of ligularia all associate well with rhododendrons and azaleas.

R. *luteum* (syn. *Azalea pontica*)

✿ May   U. H. 2.4 m (8 ft)
H4   F3-4   FCC   AGM

Unlike so many of the rhododendrons and azaleas, this is almost a native plant, so close to Britain does it originate. Eastern Europe and the Caucasus are its native habitats, but it is now naturalised in parts of the British Isles. It deserves its popularity for several reasons : the flowers come in delightful shades of yellow, varying from form to form; they are shaped like those of the honeysuckle, and are very fragrant. Its ultimate height is reached fairly quickly, and the habit is open and delicately twiggy. Pruning after flowering will keep it compact. In autumn the leaves turn to fiery red, orange and yellow before falling. *Luteum* is easily grown from seed, and is excellent for naturalising in woodland.

Rhododendron luteum growing wild in the woods.

'Oxydol'.

'Norma'.

'Persil'.

'Norma'

❀ Late May   U. H. 1.3 m (4 1/2 ft)
H4   F4   AM   AGM

Introduced in 1888, 'Norma' was given a first award three years later, but it took another seventy-eight years before a garden merit award was given. This is one of the Rustica Hybrids, so it has double flowers, narrowly tubular, and rose red in colour, and it is also scented, as well as being fully hardy. Growing slowly it is unlikely to overwhelm even a small garden, and would make a good container-plant for the terrace.

'Oxydol'

❀ May   U. H. 1.8-2.5 m (6-8 ft)   H4   F3

White as a colour, if it can be called a colour, is rarely met with in azaleas, or in rhododendrons for that matter. Such brilliantly coloured flowers as azaleas and rhododendrons are pollinated by day-flying insects, on the whole, and white may be an aberrant form of flower. Nevertheless a white azalea makes a pleasantly cool change from the orange, pink, red and salmon kinds, and the distinctive yellow blotch in the throat emphasizes the icy impression. It is a Knap Hill Hybrid.

'Persil'

❀ May   U. H. 2 m (6 1/2 ft)   H4   F4

White is a distinctive colour in the garden and 'Persil' is one of the best of the white deciduous azaleas. Its pure white flowers have a deep yellow blotch in the throat and are large for an azalea, being more than 5 cm (2 in) wide. Although included in the Knap Hill group, it is somewhat like the Ghent azaleas which often have hose-in-hose flowers amongst the single ones.

'Royal Command'

❀ May   U. H. 1.8-2.5 m (6 ft)   H4   F3

Two of the Knap Hill group, the light red of 'Royal Command' and the brilliant orange of 'Exbury Orange' form another group to catch and rivet the eye in late spring. In a little shade, such as woodland, the flowers will retain the intensity of their colours until they fall, but in sunlight, they will begin to fade long before they are finished.

'Royal Command'.

'Scarlett O'Hara'.

'Scarlett O'Hara'

❀ May   U. H. 2 m (6 1/2 ft)   H4   F1

A deep red-budded azalea, the flowers of this hybrid open to bright red, tinted yellow in the throat. The young leaves and shoots are coppery red, so the whole plant has a rather fiery appearance in May; in fact the colour is outstanding, even amongst azaleas. Height 2 m (6 1/2 ft), as with all the Knap Hill group.

'Silver Slipper'

❀ May   U. H. 1.8-2.5 m (6-8 ft)
H4   F4   FCC   AM

A charming name for a charming plant, its trumpet-shaped flowers are some of the most beautiful of the Knap Hill Hybrids, or indeed of any azalea. White with a pink flush, and with distinctive yellow markings in the throat, the flowers are accompanied by young leaves and stems tinted with reddish bronze.

'Spek's Orange'

Mid-May   U. H. 1.5 m (5 ft)
H4   F4   FCC   AM   AGM

As with the other Mollis azaleas, the brilliant orange flowers of this hybrid unfold on bare branches, but in mid-May which is later than the rest of its group. It is of Dutch origin, introduced in the late 1940s.

'Spek's Orange'.

'Silver Slipper'.

'Strawberry Ice'
✿ May   U. H. 2 m (6 1/2 ft)
H 4   F 3   AM   AGM

As one of the best azalea hybrids 'Strawberry Ice' is deservedly popular. The flower buds are red, and open to pale flesh-pink flowers, darkening to rose-pink at the edges of the petals, and paling to yellow in the throat. This plant from the Knap Hill stable would be especially charming mixed with one of the lavender-blue rhododendrons such as 'Blue Peter', which also flowers in May.

R. viscosum
✿ June-July   U. H. 4.5 m (15 ft)
H 4   F 2-3   AM   AGM

The Swamp Honeysuckle is from eastern North America, and is especially valuable for its late flowering as well as for its delicious fragrance. Sadly, it is all too rarely available in cultivation. The narrow-tubular flowers, white and sometimes flushed with pink, follow the leaves. Not surprisingly, it does best in moist soil.

Azaleodendron 'Glory of Littleworth'

❀ May/June   U. H. 1.2 m (4 ft)   H4   AM

This is an interesting hybrid from a cros
between a deciduous and evergreen azalea. Th
conspicuous flowers have a creamy colour wit
a pronounced orange blotch in the throa
The young foliage is an attractive blue-grey
and fairly frequent pruning will be required t
keep the plant compact and encourage ne
foliage.

*The brilliant reds
and purples of
Japanese azaleas
can be mellowed
by interplanting
green or variegate
hostas.*

Evergreen azaleas

*Most of this group come from Japan and consist of low growing,
compact shrubs, which are literally covered in flowers in April and May. They are generally
single-flowered, though some are 'hose-in-hose' and they do best if shaded from
the sun at some time during the day. Height is about 60-90 cm (2-3 ft). The most famous
group is the Kurume azalea group, from Japan, from which E. H. Wilson
selected and sent back in 1920 the now-famous 'Wilson's Fifty', which he considered
to be the outstanding hybrids. Other groups are the Kaempferi Hybrids,
from Holland, the Indian or Indica Hybrids, which are tender and include the indoor
pot-azaleas so often seen at Christmas, and the Vuyk Hybrids, also from Holland.*

Rose pink flowers of evergreen Azalea 'Vuyk's Rosyred' in a woodland setting.

'Atalanta'

❀ May   U. H. 65 cm - 1 m (2-3 ft)   H4   F2

One of the Dutch group of hybrids, known as the Kaempferi Hybrids, which were introduced about 1920. A delicate and fragile-looking plant with lilac flowers.

'Betty'

❀ May   U. H. 1.2 m (4 ft)   H4   F4   AM

One of the Kaempferi group, this is a strong growing hybrid, whose salmon-pink flowers have a darker centre. Its dark green foliage is an effective background for the flowers.

'Bengal Fire'
✿ May   U. H. 1.8 m (6 ft)   H4   F1   AM

A group of hybrids known as the Oldhamii Hybrids, from crosses between *R. kaempferi* and *R. oldhamii,* were produced at Exbury in the early 1930s. Their main characteristic is the size of the flowers, which are 7.5 cm (3 in) wide. 'Bengal Fire' is one of the best of this collection reaching its ultimate height after many years, average being about 1.2 m (4 ft). The flowers are a true flame-orange in colour, clothing a spreading bush, wider than it is tall, whose leaves are softly hairy.

'Blaauw's Pink'

✿ April - early May   U. H. 90 - 120 cm (3-4 ft)
H4   F3

While most azaleas have single flowers, occasionally a hybrid will have double ones, so that one flower is inside another, or is 'hose-in-hose', as some of the old-fashioned primulas are. 'Blaauw's Pink' belongs to this distinctive group, and has salmon-pink flowers. Upright in habit, it is one of the Kurume group of azaleas.

'Blue Danube'

✿ June   U. H. 90-120 cm (3-4 ft)   H4   F1

A most distinctive and unusual hybrid, whose flowers are a deep blue-violet, appearing late, For an azalea, they are large, up to 7.5 cm (3 in) wide. It is a Vuyk Hybrid, from the Vuyk van Nes Nursery in Holland; all this group appeared soon after the first world war.

'Favorite'

❀ May   U. H. 1 m (3 ft)   H 4   F 3

The Japanese evergreen azaleas can be relied on to produce a mass of bloom, and 'Favorite' will be covered in deep rosy pink flowers in early May. The dark green shining leaves make it attractive all year, and its upright but dense habit of growth is a change from the usually rather spreading plants of this group of azaleas. To 1 m (3 ft) tall, it will grow well in a sunny position.

'Fedora'

✿ May   U. H. 1.5 m (5 ft)
H4   F4   FCC   AM

This is a Kaempferi Hybrid introduced in 1922. Height is eventually 1.5 m (5 ft), though it will be about 90-120 cm (3-4 ft) for some years — growth is not rapid. The flowers are large, deep pink, and have a dark marking in the throat. *Kaempferi* itself is an evergreen or semi-deciduous azalea, whose flowers vary greatly in colour, being various shades of pink or orange-pink, sometimes double, and appearing at a variety of times, depending on the form.

'Hatsugiri'

✿ April   U. H. 60 cm (2 ft)
H4   F3   FCC   AM

A Kurume azalea which was one of the 'Wilson's Fifty', low-growing to 60 cm (2 ft), but spreading more widely, to about 90 cm (3 ft). In April, it will be a sheet of bright magenta flowers, and looks especially attractive on a rock garden. It is a twiggy little bush, completely reliable in its flowering and rightly popular.

'Fedora'.

'Hatsugiri'.

'Hinodegiri'

✤ April   U. H. 90 cm (3 ft)
H4   F4   AM   AGM

Another Kurume member of the 'Fifty', this is also one of the best in the group. It is a dense and compact bush, a little bigger than 'Hatsugiri', and 1.5 m (5 ft) wide, whose bright flowers are especially eye-catching. It often has good leaf colouring of red, bronze and orange in autumn, though the leaves do not fall.

'Hinomayo'

✤ May   U. H. 90-120 cm (3-4 ft)
H4   F4   FCC   AM   AGM

From the Emperor's garden in Tokyo, this was the first Japanese azalea to be brought to Europe, in the early part of this century. Its exceedingly . pretty, delicately pink flowers cover a bush seen at its best if grown in dappled shade.

'Hinomayo'.

'Hinodegiri'.

'Iro-hayama'
❀ May   U. H. 45 cm (1/2 ft)   H 4   F 4

A small plant but wide at 105 cm (3 1/2 ft), this azalea has light-green leaves and white flowers edged with lavender, making it a pleasing and unusual hybrid of the Kurume group.

'John Cairns'
❀ May   U. H. 90-120 cm (3-4 ft)
H 4   F 4   AM   AGM

This is a Kaempferi cross, very hardy, and not always completely evergreen. Wider than tall, it will spread to about 1.5 m (5 ft) after many years, and performs the miracle in late spring of producing a mass of dark orange-red flowers completely hiding the leaves. In autumn the leaves are tinted red sufficiently strongly to make it a 'two-season' shrub.

'Kirin'

❀ May   U. H. 1 m (3 ft)
H3   F4   AM   AGM

As this is one of the Wilson Kurumes, 'Kirin' is naturally an outstandingly pretty azalea. Its flowers are 'hose-in-hose', and are deep rose-pink on the outside, lighter silvery-pink on the inside. Height is eventually about 1 m (3 ft) and flowering is in early May. It is not quite hardy, so needs care in placing, and is often sold as a pot plant, being forced for flowering in January and February.

An effective garden group with the brilliant red Azalea 'Hinodegiri' and a specimen green cut-leaf Japanese maple. The small white flowers are Rhododendron 'Trichostomum'.

'Malvaticum'

❀ May-June   U. H. 90 cm (3 ft)   H4   F1

This is a seedling from 'Hinodegiri' raised about 1910, and still a good, strong plant, wide-spreading and about 90 cm (3 ft) tall. Large purple flowers streaked and spotted with deeper purple, appear rather late, in May and June.

'Mother's Day'

❀ June   U. H. 1 / 2.5 m (3/7 1/2 ft)
H4   F4   AM   AGM

Given both the Award of Merit and the Award of Garden Merit, this is one of the very best dwarf evergreen azaleas, resulting from a cross between a Kurume hybrid and an Indian azalea. The flowers are large semi double dark red and appear in late May to early June, generally avoiding the late spring frost. The foliage is also an attractive red bronze colour.

'Orange Beauty'
✿ May   U. H. 1.2 m (4 ft)
H4   F4   FCC   AM   AGM

The mass of awards that this hybrid has received speak for themselves, as does its name, and it is certainly one of the most popular of the evergreen azaleas. The salmon-orange flowers are a glorious colour, produced in May on a plant slowly growing to about 1.2 m (4 ft). The hairy leaves are large for an azalea, and the oldest become tinted with red in autumn for some weeks, before they eventually fall.

'Palestrina'
✿ May   U. H. 1.2 m (4 ft)
H4   F4   AM   AGM   FCC

Deservedly winning all these awards, the Dutch hybrid 'Palestrina' has starkly white, funnel-shaped flowers with green flashes in the throat. It blooms in May. Habit tends to be rather upright, to about 1.2 m (4 ft). Although evergreen, it loses some of its leaves in winter, but they are quickly replaced with new ones in spring.

'Purple Splendour'

✿ May　U. H. 1.2 m (4 ft)　H4　F3

From the Vuyk van Nes Nursery of Holland,
'Purple Splendour' has distinctive reddish-
purple blooms and each one is quite large,
up to 7.5 cm (3 in) wide. These large flowers
intensify the colour effect and really do make
the plant a splendid specimen in May.

'Rosebud'

✿ May　U. H. 1.5 m (5 ft)　H4　F3　AM

A very distinctive azalea with large double
pink flowers, when fully grown it forms a low
rather spreading bush. 'Rosebud' can be forced
into early flower and is quite often sold as
a winter pot plant. A very interesting variety
for a small garden.

'Satsuki'
✿ April   U. H. 45 cm (1 1/2 ft)   H4   F3

The so-called Indian azaleas are mostly tender plants, used for forcing to be in flower at Christmas, and all are extremely pretty. 'Satsuki' is one of the hardier ones which can be grown outdoors in a sheltered place, and is dwarf, growing only to 45 cm (1 1/2 ft). The pink, open funnel-shaped flowers, 7.5 cm (3 in) wide, have a dark blotch in the throat, and are produced in profusion all over the plant, in April.

'Snow'
✿ May   U. H. 90 cm (3 ft)   H4   F3

As might be expected, the flowers of this hybrid are pure white, accentuated by a green tinge in the throat. They are generally double, or 'hose-in-hose', but sometimes come singly. Height of this Kurume azalea is about 90 cm (3 ft).

Red and pink azaleas massed together in th Devil's Punch Bowl, a beauty spot near Hindhea

'Vuyk's Rosyred'

✿ May U.H. 1.2 m (4 ft) H4 F4 AM

Low and spreading, about 1.5 m (5 ft) wide this has very large flowers, 7.8 cm (3 in) wide or more, light red with a deeper marking in the throat.

'Vuyk's Rosyred'.

'Vuyk's Scarlet' with *Pieris forrestii*
⚘ May   U. H. 80 cm (2 1/2 ft)   H4   F4   FCC   AM   AGM

The brilliantly deep red, large flowers of this azalea, with their frilly edges, take a lot of beating for beauty, and its compact habit and short stature 80 cm (32 in) make it indispensable for the small garden, or rock garden. Flowering is in May. In this illustration it is associated with another acid-loving shrub, whose young growth is brilliantly red also, but lighter in tone, *Pieris forrestii*. Sprays of white, lily-of-the-valley flowers are produced by the pieris, also in May, and the two plants are splendid companions.

Evergreen azaleas by the lake in Exbury Gardens.

Camellias

The camellias are amongst the prettiest flowering shrubs that
can be grown in a temperate climate, such as that of Britain. All the C. japonica
forms can be grown outdoors, and will survive considerable frost,
even to the extent of being covered in icicles; the sasanqua
and reticulata kinds are, however, rather more tender, but will live outdoors
in a very mild, sheltered garden. March and April are the main
flowering months for japonica and reticulata.
Sasanqua kinds start in November and continue through the winter;
also they are the only kinds that are fragant. The flower form
of camellia ranges from the single flower with eight or nine petals only,
through the anemone- and peony-flowered,
which have a bunched-up centre of many petals decreasing in size
until they are petaloids, to the final type which is fully double,
and completely formal, with overlapping petals right through to the centre,
and no stamens. Flower colour is in the pink, red, rose,
carmine and white part of the spectrum, sometimes marbled
and streaked, and the final height of the plants is anything
from 2.1 m to 4.5 m (8-15 ft), but they are not quick growers,
putting on only about 15-22 cm (6-9 in) a year.
Most of the available camellias are sports, mutations or selections
of japonica and the other species mentioned. However, there are some hybrids,
resulting from the williamsii cross of saluenensis and japonica;
these are singles and generally very free-flowering, with names like
'Donation', 'Citation' and 'Salutation', etc.

A fine
specimen
of early
flowering
Camellia
'St. Ewe'
in a woodland
setting.

111

'Adolphe Audusson'

One of the most beautiful of the camellias, th
blood-red petals of this cultivar are perfectl
set off by the clustered yellow stamens in thei
centre. To 3 m (10 ft) tall, and about 2.4 m (8 ft
wide, it is upright but compact in habit, reaso
nably vigorous and reliable in its flowering eacl
year, in April.

'Alba Simplex'

AGM

White-flowered camellias have a purity unri
valled by any other flower, perhaps because o
the bright green, shining leaves which set then
off to perfection. 'Alba Simplex' has large
single flowers, centred with a conspicuou
cluster of golden stamens. It will grow in tim
into a large bushy plant, about 6 m (20 ft) tall
All white camellias are, unfortunately, pron
to spring frost-damage to the flowers, so a
position which is unlikely to be subject to ai
frosts should be chosen.

'Chandlerii Elegans'

FCC   AM   AGM

Deep rosy-pink flowers marked with white, appear on this plant in March and early April. The very large flowers have the anemone form, and are slow to open; it is an accommodating camellia which will grow in almost any garden, forming a low, spreading bush.

'Chardonneret'

This hybrid was introduced in 1975 by Thoby. It has imbricated flowers completely round, pale pink and marbled with carmine in places. It grows strongly and is well-shaped. Flowers in February-March.

'Contessa Lavinia Maggi'

FCC   AGM

The Contessa is one of the oldest cultivated forms, being given a first award in 1862. The flower is formal, completely double, and beautifully shaped so that the petals exactly alternate in each rank; they are pale pink, splashed and striped with red. Besides a good shape and colour, the flowers are large, and freely produced in early April, covering a shapely plant of about 3 m (10 ft) in height after ten years.

Camellia Seed Pods.

Camellias frequently produce attractive pods in the autumn containing shiny black seeds. These will germinate and produce new plants, but as the majority of Camellias are hybrids the seedlings will produce flowers of uncertain colour, and are often very shy flowering.

'Debbie'
AM

A new hybrid, introduced from New Zealand in 1965 - it shows every sign of being an excellent and exciting camellia. As well as being vigorous and upright in growth, the peony-form flowers are large, 10 cm (4 in) wide, freely produced, and a glowing rose-pink. 'Debbie' can be relied on to flower every year, starting early in March and continuing through April. Much work on hybridization of camellias is being undertaken in New Zealand, and some really beautiful hardy hybrids are being produced, the colour, size and form of whose flowers is outstanding. Two other exceptionally attractive camellias from New Zealand are 'Elsie Jury', whose 13 cm (5 in) flowers are anemone-centred, and 'Anticipation', a deep crimson, double-flowered camellia.

'Duchess de Caze'

This vigorous plant moderately free flowering, carries extraordinary peony-formed flowers in January to February, pale pink turning to white on the edges of the petals, and marbled with a deeper pink. It is useful for cut flowers.

Camellia 'Donation' grown in a tub, giving an excellent display of colour.

'Donation'

A most beautiful camellia, the large, semi-double, orchid-pink flowers are profusely produced on a vigorous bush in April. It can remain in flower for a month, and all the praise and publicity it has had are more than justified. 'Donation' is probably the most popular, and possibly the loveliest camellia produced this century - it even has the merit of flowering while a very young plant, only a few inches high. Habit is erect and compact, and it may grow to 4.5 m (15 ft) tall in time.

'Gloire de Nantes'

An old and famous hybrid from the end of 19 th century,
introduced by Henri Guichard. Its large, semi-double flowers display to great effect the pink petals
which are veined with a deeper pink, and which half conceal a mass of golden stamens.
It is a plant of average foliage but it has a graceful habit and is very floriferous.

'Golden Spangles'

The bright shiny green camellia foliage is attractive all the year round, 'Golden Spangles' has the distinction of unusual leaves with a central yellow-green blotch, the single pink flowers appear in early spring, making a striking contrast against the foliage. A fairly sheltered site in the garden will suit this camellia best to avoid sun or wind damage to the foliage.

'Golden Spangles'.

'Hippolyte Thoby'.

'Hippolyte Thoby'

This lovely hybrid with imbricated flowers of a bright red was introduced in 1973 by Thoby. The plant is well branched and compact and very floriferous, and is suitable for container growing. It flowers at the end of winter.

'Inspiration'

A camellia whose flowers are like a more intensely-pink 'Donation', semi-double, with deep green foliage to offset them. The plant is moderately spreading, and flowers in March, or earlier in sheltered gardens, due to its reticulata blood. *C. reticulata* is the Chinese equivalent of *C. japonica* from Japan, and is thought to be somewhat tender, but in fact the hybrids are perfectly hardy most winters, in most gardens.

Opposite page : 'Inspiration'

'Lady Clare'

AM AGM

Although this had an award given to it as long ago as 1927,
it is still one of the best camellias, because of its beauty of flower and vigour of
constitution. The large, partly double flowers are peach-pink,
on an open spreading bush with an almost weeping habit. Flowering time is April.

'Leonard Messel'.

'Lady Vansittart'

For those who like the colouring of their garden plants variegated, this camellia will be specially welcome. Basically white, its wavy-edged petals are striped rose-pink in general, but the same plant may carry all-white and all-pink flowers on it, as well as the bi-coloured ones. The leaves are large and tend to be undulating. It is not a rapid grower, indeed rather the opposite, with an upright habit. Flowering is in April; height is 3-3.6 m (10-12 ft).

'Leonard Messel'
FCC AM

The original of this beautiful camellia can be seen in the National Trust garden at Nymans, Sussex, and it was produced by crossing the species *Camellia reticulata* with the *williamsii* hybrid 'Mary Christian'. The habit is rather open, and in time the plant can grow into a small tree, generously adorned with partly double, clear pink flowers in early spring. The flowers are large, as much as 10 cm (4 in) wide, and sometimes marked with white marbling.

'Lady Vansittart'.

'Madame Charles Blard'

This magnificent hybrid was introduced in 1920 by Guichard.
It has wonderful peony-form flowers in March to April, of a pure white shaded yellow
at the base of the petals. Its habit is somewhat weeping.

'Magnoliiflora'
AM

Fairly small pale pink flowers with attractive pointed petals similar to a miniature water lily. Usually a very free flowering camellia in April-May, and what is lost in the size of flowers is gained in the quality.

'Margherita Coleoni'

Its large glossy leaves make a good foil for the large, round imbricated flowers which are a fairly dark red. It has a well-shaped form.

'Mathotiana Rosea'

A large imbricated flower, bright pink, appearing at the end of the season, towards March to April. Its leaves are large and of a luminous green. The plant is also large but its roots are less fibrous than usual which makes transplanting a risky operation.

'Nobillissima'

Double white flowers with a hint of yellow are very effective against the dark green, shiny foliage. This is one of the earliest camellias to bloom in spring and needs a sheltered position to avoid frost damage. The plant has a rather upright habit.

'Preston Rose'
AGM

The form of camellia flowers may be single with no more than eight or nine petals, or the flower may be double and consist of a rather untidy mass of petals and petaloids; the latter is called 'peony flowered', and 'Preston Rose' is one of these, coloured salmon-pink. It is a strongly-growing, upright plant flowering in April.

'St Ewe' (Williamsii)
AM

The *williamsii* hybrids have the merit of starting to flower as early as November, but only in warm, sheltered gardens, and will then flower intermittently through the winter until their main season in spring. This is a charming plant, with cup-like rosy pink flowers, seen at their best if the plant is given a lightly-wooded setting.

'Preston Rose'.

'St Ewe'.

'Tricolor'

The flowers have a base colour of white or pink
with prominent carmine streaks. In full flower this well-
proven camellia is very distinctive.

Principal gardens to visit
for rhododendrons, azaleas & camellias

Bodnant Gardens, Tal-y-cafyn, Gwynedd,
Borde Hill Gardens, Nr. Haywards Heath, West Sussex.
Brodick Castle, Isle of Arran, Bute.
Exbury Gardens, Exbury, Southampton.
Hilliers Arboretum, Ampfield, Hampshire.
Kew Gardens, Kew, London.
Knightshayes Court, Tiverton, Devon.
Leonardslee, Nr. Horsham, West Sussex.
Royal Horticultural Gardens, Wisley, Nr. Guildford, Surrey.
Savill Gardens and Valley Gardens, Windsor Great Park, Berkshire.
Trewithen Gardens, Nr. Truro, Cornwall.
Wakehurst Place, Ardingly, West Sussex.

BACK COVER :
Massed yellow azaleas in a cool woodland setting.

INSIDE BACK COVER :
A brilliant display of mixed Exbury azaleas. Massed in a border they make excellent ground cover.

Index

Printed in France   © ÉDITIONS FLORAISSE, all rights reserved - Second edition - Legally deposed n° 274 MARCH 1984